CONTENTS

What is Sanctification?

Scripturally, the word =sanctification= has three meanings: First, separation; second, dedication; third, spirit-filling. Webster's definition of it is as follows: "1. Sanctification is the act of God's grace by which the affections of man are purified, or alienated from sin and the world, and exalted to a supreme love of God; also, the state of being thus purified or sanctified. 2. The act of consecrating, or setting apart for a sacred purpose." "=Sanctifier.= One who sanctifies or makes holy; specifically, the Holy Ghost." "=Sanctify.= 1. To set apart to a holy or religious use. 2. To make holy or free from sin; to cleanse from moral corruption or pollution; to make holy by detaching the affections from the world and its defilements and exalting them to a supreme love of God." Scripturally and practically, the terms sanctification, holiness, purity, and perfection are synonymous. =Holiness=, Separation: setting apart; sacredness. =Purity.= Cleanness; chastity. =Perfection.= Completeness; wholeness. All this is comprehended in one word, =sanctification=.

It is evident that this term signifies much more in the New Testament sense than it does in the Old Testament. In the Old Testament it meant but a dedication, a setting apart to a holy use, as in the example of the sanctification of the tabernacle and its contents--the altar and laver, and all the vessels belonging thereto--and Aaron and his sons and their garments. Lev. 8:10-30. In this dispensation of grace it means infinitely more; for in that dispensation it was but an outward and ceremonial work, but now it is an inwrought work, permeating and purifying the affections through and through by the cleansing blood and heavenly fire, and filling the dedicated temple, our body, with the Holy Ghost, as in the example of the early church at Pentecost.

The justified believer must meet the conditions of complete separation and exclusive dedication of himself to God, in a sense that no guilty sinner can do. This is the believer's part. He must purify himself. "Every man that hath this hope in him purifieth himself, even as he is pure."--1 John 3:3. "Having therefore these promises, dearly beloved, let us cleanse ourselves from all filthiness of the flesh and spirit, perfecting holiness in the fear of God."--2 Cor.

7:1. This brings the believer into the condition where God can fulfill his part. He can now take exclusive possession of the dedicated temple, and sanctify it. "And the very God of peace sanctify you wholly."--1 Thess. 5:23. "And they were all filled with the Holy Ghost."--Acts 2:4. This brings the believer into a more perfect spiritual relationship with God than when simply justified.

Sanctification A Bible Doctrine

"And now, brethren, I commend you to God, and to the word of his grace, which is able to build you up, and to give you an inheritance among all them which are sanctified." Acts 20:32.

"To open their eyes, and to turn them from darkness to light, and from the power of Satan unto God, that they may receive forgiveness of sins, and inheritance among them which are sanctified by faith that is in me."--Acts 26:18.

"Sanctify them through thy truth: thy word is truth.... And for their sakes I sanctify myself, that they also might be sanctified through the truth. Neither pray I for these alone, but for them also which shall believe on me through their word."--John 17:17, 19, 20.

"If a man therefore purge himself from these, he shall be a vessel unto honour, sanctified, and meet for the master's use, and prepared unto every good work."--2 Tim. 2:21.

"That every one of you should know how to possess his vessel in sanctification and honour."--1 Thess. 4:4.

God Our Sanctifier

"And the very God of peace sanctify you wholly; and I pray God your whole spirit and soul and body be preserved blameless unto the coming of our Lord Jesus Christ. Faithful is he that calleth you, who also will do it."--1 Thess. 5:23,

24.

"Jude, the servant of Jesus Christ, and brother of James, to them that are sanctified by God the Father, and preserved in Jesus Christ, and called."--Jude 1.

Sanctified In Christ

"Unto the church of God which is at Corinth, to them that are sanctified in Christ Jesus." "But of him are ye in Christ Jesus, who of God is made unto us wisdom, and righteousness, and sanctification, and redemption."--1 Cor. 1:2, 30.

Sanctified Through the Truth

"Sanctify them through thy truth; thy word is truth."--John 17:17. "That he might sanctify and cleanse it with the washing of water by the word."--Eph. 5:26.

By The Blood of Jesus

"Wherefore Jesus also, that he might sanctify the people with his own blood, suffered without the gate." "For if the blood of bulls and of goats, and the ashes of an heifer sprinkling the unclean, sanctifieth to the purifying of the flesh: how much more shall the blood of Christ, who through the eternal Spirit offered himself without spot to God, purge your conscience from dead works to serve the living God?" "By the which will we are sanctified through the offering of the body of Jesus Christ once for all." "For by one offering he hath perfected for ever them that are sanctified."

"Of how much sorer punishment, suppose ye, shall he be thought worthy, who hath trodden under foot the Son of God, and hath counted the blood of the covenant, wherewith he was sanctified, an unholy thing, and hath done despite unto the Spirit of grace?"--Heb. 13:12; 9:13, 14; 10:10, 14, 29.

And The Holy Spirit

"That I should be the minister of Jesus Christ to the Gentiles, ministering the gospel of God, that the offering up of the Gentiles might be acceptable, being sanctified by the Holy Ghost."--Rom. 15:16. "But we are bound to give thanks alway to God for you, brethren beloved of the Lord, because God hath from the beginning chosen you to salvation through sanctification of the Spirit and belief of the truth."--2 Thess. 2:13.

These and many other texts of scripture teach us that sanctification is a Bible doctrine. There is but one reason why some people can not see it in the Bible-- their eyes are blinded. All who are willing to yield themselves to God and His word, will soon be taught this blessed truth. Jesus prayed that His disciples might become sanctified. They had not yet come into this experience. Jesus knew that they needed it. It was His desire for their highest good. They were not able to go forth and cope with the powers of sin. They had been under the teaching of the Master and in His presence, and therefore were protected by Him from the enemy; but now he was soon to be taken from them, and He knew that they must be "endued with power from on high." Therefore He implored the Father for the sanctification of the eleven; and not "for these alone," but "for them also which shall believe on me through their word." This reaches down through the entire gospel dispensation. It is His blessed will that we all shall be sanctified. As justified believers, we each are as needy of this grace as were the eleven disciples. It is indispensable for our spiritual welfare.

Some are disposed to look upon this matter as optional with them; but such is a mistake. The time comes in the experience of every true believer when the Holy Spirit brings before him the conditions of a definite and absolute consecration. A refusal to meet these conditions, done ignorantly, will bring a cloud over our experience of justification and, eventually, if persisted in wilfully, will bring us into God's utter disapproval. "Therefore to him that knoweth to do good, and doeth it not, to him it is sin."--Jas. 4:17.

Sanctification is the normal state of the Christian. The Father, Son and Holy Spirit are jointly interested in us, that we attain unto this grace. Our unity with the Godhead is incomplete without it, so also is our unity with each other; "For both he that sanctifieth and they who are sanctified are all of one: for which cause he is not ashamed to call them brethren."--Heb. 2:11. A heart washed and made pure by the blood of Christ and filled with the Holy Spirit will always be in perfect fellowship with divinity, and also with all other hearts of like experience. The unsanctified heart of the believer cannot be fully satisfied, because of the consciousness of the presence of the carnal nature, more scripturally called "our old man." Just what it is may not perhaps be perfectly understood by the new convert, but that something abnormal exists will soon be discovered, and there will be a longing in the heart for an inward cleansing--a normal desire for the normal experience. On the other hand, when this blessed experience is attained, there comes with it the consciousness of inward purity which fully satisfies the heart, and it can sing with the spirit and with the understanding, "Hallelujah for the cleansing; it has reached my inmost soul."

For this purpose Christ gave himself for the church--"That he might sanctify and cleanse it." God gave him to the world that whosoever believes in him shall not perish, but have everlasting life, for our justification; but Christ gave himself for the church, for our sanctification.

The gospel commission of the apostle Paul specifies clearly the doctrine of sanctification, the "inheritance among them which are sanctified." He could not have been faithful to this commission without leading souls from "forgiveness of sins" into this "inheritance." His ministry and epistles to the different churches prove his faithfulness. Upon his first acquaintance with the brethren at Ephesus he asked them the question, "Have ye received the Holy Ghost since ye believed?" And after three years of faithful ministry in that city, upon the solemn event of his departure from them, among his last words he reminds the church of the "inheritance among all them which are sanctified." Then about four years later, while a prisoner at Rome, he writes back to them his epistle to the Ephesians, which in every chapter sparkles with beautiful gems of thought upon the subject of sanctification. In his letter to the church of Rome we are forcibly reminded that this doctrine was prominent in his teaching, employing such terms as, "this grace wherein we stand" (Rom. 5:2), "our old man is crucified," "that the body of sin might be destroyed," "dead indeed unto sin," "free from sin" (Chap. 6), "married to ... him who is raised from the dead" (Chap. 7), "present your bodies a living sacrifice" (Chap. 12) "being sanctified by the Holy Ghost" (Chap. 15). These terms and others signify the precious experiences of sanctification.

In the first and second epistles to the Corinthians we also notice the mention of this experience, and that there were some saints at Corinth that were sanctified (1:2, 30), although some were not, and were told that they were yet carnal. There were evidently only the two classes--sanctified and justified, in the church there, the same as is usually the case everywhere today. In speaking of the congregation, he says "But ye are washed, but ye are sanctified, but ye are justified in the name of the Lord Jesus, and by the Spirit of God."--1 Cor. 6:11. In the second epistle, Chap. 7:1, he exhorts them: "Let us cleanse ourselves from all filthiness of the flesh and spirit, perfecting holiness in the fear of God," and among the closing words of this letter, he says, "Be perfect."

Thus we can see in all the epistles of this apostle, the theme of sanctification. His personal testimony to the Galatians reads: "I am crucified with Christ." His statement to the brethren at Philippi was: "As many as be perfect"; to those at Colosse: "Ye are dead and your life is hid with Christ in God," "Ye have put off the old man with his deeds, and have put on the new man"; his teaching in the epistles to the Thessalonians, showing them that sanctification is the will of God to them, and his desire that the "God of peace sanctify you wholly." His instructions to Timothy show how we may become a vessel "sanctified and meet for the Master's use," and he refers to the fact that there were some who "call on the Lord out of a pure heart." His letter to Titus, in which he mentions how Jesus gave himself for us, that he might "purify unto himself a peculiar people." These all add testimony to this doctrine and the apostle's faithfulness in his ministry. Some scholars think Apollos is the author of the epistle to the Hebrews; but whether Paul or Apollos, it abounds with truth upon sanctification.

All the other writers of the New Testament teach the same truth. James says, "Purify your hearts, ye double-minded." Peter gives emphasis to the doctrine of holiness: "Be ye holy," and that "we, being dead to sins, should live unto righteousness"; and desires that the God of all grace "make you perfect, stablish, strengthen, settle you;" and that at the coming of Christ "ye may be found of him in peace, without spot and blameless." Jude addresses his epistle "to them that are sanctified," and "preserved."

Then when we search the writings of John we are almost overwhelmed with glory, as we read his beautiful teachings upon this theme, which he so clearly sets forth. God grant that we all may "walk in the light as he is in the light," walking "even as he walked," that his love in us may be "perfected," that we may prayerfully hold fast and abide in this "unction from the Holy One," that the "anointing" may abide in us. Such an experience can be realized only by every one that "purifieth himself even as he is pure."

CHAPTER II

The Apostolic Experience

"All scripture is given by inspiration of God, and is profitable for doctrine, for reproof, for correction, for instruction in righteousness: that the man of God may be perfect, thoroughly furnished unto all good works."--2 Tim. 3:16, 17.

In our study of this theme we find that the word of God is our only standard to prove that sanctification is a Bible doctrine. The experience and testimony of the Bible writers and the other apostles of the early church also prove to us and teach the nature of this doctrine and its relative position to the experience of justification. It will be important and profitable for us to review these experiences, not only to establish the doctrine in our faith, but also to examine our own hearts and see that our experiences are truly apostolic.

The author of this treatise was sanctified at a time when there was a battle raging against the doctrine as a second work of grace. He had himself taken a stand against it for some years, because it did not seem that the scriptures and apostolic testimonies were sufficiently clear to establish the second-work doctrine. In this he had been blinded by the theories on the opposing side, notwithstanding the brilliant testimonies to the contrary of those whose lives were unimpeachable. Of course it was impossible to consecrate for and receive the experience under such circumstances, and consequently years of unsatisfactory experience passed by, until at last the indisputable symptoms of inborn depravity, and the deplorable weakness of the heart and will to cope with the mighty power of the enemy, brought the struggling soul into depths of despair at the feet of Jesus, crying, "Forgive me, O Lord, for all my sad failures, and 'create in me a clean heart, O God.'" It was not a question at this crisis about it being a second work of grace. The crying need of the soul was a clean heart. It was all too evident that the heart was not clean, and it was also evident that it was the will of God, even my sanctification; and dear loved ones were daily proving by life and testimony that the experience was attainable.

It will be sufficient to say at present that the definite consecration and definite faith in the definite promises of God brought the definite experience. The inward struggle was over, and the soul had entered into its promised land--the heavenly rest; "for we which have believed do enter into rest."--Heb. 4:3. Experimentally, the question of the second work was most thoroughly and satisfactorily answered, and it seemed as clear as the noonday sun in a cloudless sky. The internal evidence was overwhelming, and now it only remained necessary to become established scripturally, which, by the study of the apostolic experiences and testimonies, was by the anointing received in due time. Praise God!

Were it not for the perverted teaching, every truly justified child of God would soon be led by the Holy Spirit into this grace, because it is the inheritance of the soul, and its normal state. The apostles before Pentecost needed it, and so does every other child of God. Let us briefly consider the experience of the apostolic brethren, both before and upon their Pentecost.

=They were born of God before Pentecost.= This is very definitely established by the following scriptures. "Whosoever believeth that Jesus is the Christ is born of God"--1 John 5:1. "He saith unto them, But whom say ye that I am? And Simon Peter answered and said, Thou art the Christ, the Son of the living God."--Matt. 16:15, 16. "But as many as received him, to them gave he power to become the sons of God, even to them that believe on his name: which were born, not of blood, nor of the will of the flesh, nor of the will of man, but of God."--John 1:12, 13. "Nathanael answered and saith unto him, Rabbi, thou art the Son of God."--John 1:49. "Then saith he to Thomas, Reach hither thy finger, and behold my hands; and reach hither thy hand, and thrust it into my side; and be not faithless, but believing. And Thomas answered and said unto him, My Lord and my God. Jesus saith unto him, Thomas, because thou hast seen me, thou hast believed: blessed are they that have not seen, and yet have believed."--John 20:27-29.

This is sufficient to prove their experience, both before and after the death and resurrection of Christ. Some would contend that the disciples could not have been regenerated in a true New Testament sense before Pentecost, because the plan of salvation was not finished before Christ's death on the cross. If this were true, there is sufficient in the foregoing text (John 20:27-29) to prove that the eleven were enjoying the regenerating grace; for they all had at least as much faith as Thomas, that Jesus is the Christ; and when Thomas was invited to prove to his own satisfaction that Jesus had indeed risen from the dead, he at once acknowledged him "My Lord and my God." This was after the atonement for sin was made, and the disciples believed in him and beyond doubt were justified and born of God in the perfect New Testament sense. This not only is true of the eleven, but equally so of all who believed that he arose from the dead; for he said, "Blessed are they that have not seen and yet have believed."

The language of the apostle to the Roman brethren (Chap. 10:9, 10) adds to this testimony--"That if thou shalt confess with thy mouth the Lord Jesus, and shalt believe in thine heart that God hath raised him from the dead, thou shalt be saved. For with the heart man believeth unto righteousness; and with the mouth confession is made unto salvation." The apostle John says (1 John 2:29), "If ye know that he is righteous, ye know that every one that doeth righteousness is born of him." He also says, "Every one that loveth is born of God, and knoweth God."--1 John 4:7.

=Their names were written in heaven.= "Notwithstanding in this rejoice not, that the spirits are subject unto you; but rather rejoice, because your names are written in heaven."--Luke 10:20. The critic will say that this was said of the seventy and not of the twelve. Well, it was said of the seventy, but how could it be less true of the twelve whom he had previously chosen and sent out to preach the kingdom of God, to cast out devils, and to heal the sick? It is likely that a number of those seventy, if not all, were among the one hundred twenty at Pentecost. To say the least concerning the spiritual standing of the twelve, they were equal with the seventy.

=They were not of the world.= "If ye were of the world, the world would love his own: but because ye are not of the world, but I have chosen you out of the world, therefore the world hateth you."--John 15:19. "I have given them thy word; and the world hath hated them, because they are not of the world, even as I am not of the world.... They are not of the world, even as I am not of the world." John 17:14,16.

=They kept the word of God.= "I have manifested thy name unto the men which thou gavest me out of the world: thine they were, and thou gavest them me; and they have kept thy word. For I have given unto them the words which thou gavest me; and they have received them, and have known surely that I came out from thee, and they have believed that thou didst send me."--John 17:6, 8.

=They belonged to God.= "I pray for them: I pray not for the world, but for them which thou hast given me; for they are thine. All mine are thine, and thine are mine; and I am glorified in them."--John 17:9, 10.

This was the spiritual condition of the eleven before Pentecost testified to by Jesus himself. It is certainly a blessed condition--born of God, their names written in heaven, not of the world. They belonged to God, and they kept His word. Would that every professing follower of Jesus were in this blessed state. It would produce a revolution in Christendom. Does not this signify all that can possibly be comprehended in justification?

Then after the blood of Jesus had been shed and the ransom for sin paid, he opened their understanding (Luke 24:45) that they might understand the scriptures, how he should suffer and rise again from the dead. We see that they believed in him the Redeemer, and now understood the object of his suffering and death; but there was still a glorious work of grace awaiting them, to be inwrought by the Holy Ghost, the sanctifier.

=They were not yet sanctified=, and for this reason Jesus prayed for them as he did. He well knew that they could not be kept from the evil of the world in a manner that would prove satisfactory to themselves and the Father, unless there should be accomplished in them more than had yet been done. Therefore he prayed, "Sanctify them through thy truth, thy word is truth."--John 17:17.

=They had not yet received the Holy Ghost.= "And, behold, I send the promise of my Father upon you: but tarry ye in the city of Jerusalem, until ye be endued with power from on high."--Luke 24:49. "For John truly baptized with water: but ye shall be baptized with the Holy Ghost not many days hence."

=This promise was fulfilled.= "And when the day of Pentecost was fully come, they were all with one accord in one place. And suddenly there came a sound from heaven as of a rushing mighty wind, and it filled all the house where they were sitting. And there appeared unto them cloven tongues like as of fire, and it sat upon each of them. And they were all filled with the Holy Ghost."--Acts 2:1-4.

We will presently consider the testimony of the apostle Peter with reference to this experience at Pentecost, but will first notice the experience of

Cornelius And His Household

This brother was a devout man; he feared God with all his house; he prayed to God always and gave much alms, which were accepted of God and were had in remembrance in his sight; he had a good report. God heard his prayers, accepted him, and answered his prayers; and he and his household were all anxious to hear the preaching of Peter, testifying, "Now therefore are we all here present before God, to hear all things that are commanded thee of God."-- Acts 10:33.

This was not a company of sinners. Peter did not preach repentance to them. Although they were Gentiles and did not have the privileges that many others had and were not acquainted with the apostles, they were acquainted with God. Peter expressed his surprise at this, saying, "Of a truth, I perceive that God is no respecter of persons: but in every nation he that feareth him, and worketh righteousness, is accepted with him." Acts 10:34, 35. Here Peter testifies both to the righteousness and to the acceptance with God of this household.

From Peter's statement in Acts 11:14, in his testimony to the church concerning this event, a doubt might arise as to this company being saved in the full New Testament justification. He refers to the words of the angel in his message to Cornelius, instructing him to send for Peter, "Who shall teach thee words whereby thou and all thy house shall be saved." But this statement in itself cannot be interpreted to mean that this company were not already justified. We have a parallel statement of Peter in his testimony to the church upon another occasion, when he again refers to the grace of God to the Gentile world, saying (Acts 15:10, 11), "Now therefore why tempt ye God, to put a yoke upon the neck of the disciples, which neither our fathers nor we were able to bear? But we believe that through the grace of the Lord Jesus Christ we shall be saved, even as they." The term "saved" in both these instances signifies more than justification; for truly Peter and the disciples to whom he was speaking in this last instance were justified.

The household of Cornelius were ready with open hearts to receive all that God had for them, and while Peter spoke the word of God to them "the Holy Ghost fell on all them which heard the word." This experience was identical in character with that of the Jewish saints at Pentecost.

Peter's Testimony

In rehearsing this wonderful event to the brethren and apostles at Jerusalem he testified to the unquestionable leading of the Spirit to this company of believers. He said (Acts 11:15, 17), "And as I began to speak, the Holy Ghost fell on them, as on us at the beginning. Forasmuch then as God gave them the like gift as he did unto us, who believed on the Lord Jesus Christ; what was I, that I could withstand God?" Upon another occasion at Jerusalem Peter again spoke of the same event, saying, "And God, which knoweth the hearts, bare them witness, giving them the Holy Ghost, even as he did unto us; and put no difference between us and them, purifying their hearts by faith."--Acts 15:8, 9. But Peter testified to the fact that the Gentiles are placed upon a level with the Jews, not only in the reception of the Holy Spirit, but in the experience of cleansing. He testified to these two phases of sanctification, equally wrought in the hearts of the Jews and Gentiles, making "no difference between us and them"; and in this same testimony he plainly states that "purifying their hearts" was an experience co-incident with the reception of the Holy Ghost--"giving them the Holy Ghost," "purifying their hearts," "even as he did unto us." Opposers of this truth have argued that Peter's statement, "purifying their hearts," in the Greek text reads, "having purified their hearts," the word "having" signifying that their hearts were purified previous to the event of their reception of the Holy Ghost; but this objection has no foundation in scripture, history, or experience. If there could be a shadow of meaning in this form of this word in the Greek text, to signify that the "purifying their hearts" occurred prior to the outpouring of the Holy Ghost, it simply has reference to the order of these two phases of sanctification, which were effected within them upon this occasion.

It is evident that in the divine order of sanctification purifying the heart by faith is preparatory to the outpouring of the Holy Spirit. He must have a pure heart in which to make his abode. However, there is no lapse of time perceptible between the =negative= and =positive= phase of sanctification. How easily this is understood by those who have truly received the Pentecostal experience. How the "anointing" teaches us and witnesses in our hearts to the testimony of Peter; but to those who have not yet had their Pentecost, and especially such as are blinded by theory and the doctrines of men, there is likely to be discussion and argument of words. The apostles and brethren at Jerusalem had no argument to make when Peter rehearsed his experience. They simply "glorified God."

Paul's Testimony

"Nevertheless, brethren, I have written the more boldly unto you in some sort, as putting you in mind, because of the grace that is given to me of God, that I should be the minister of Jesus Christ to the Gentiles, ministering the gospel of God, that the offering up of the Gentiles might be acceptable, being sanctified by the Holy Ghost."--Romans 15:15, 16.

This testimony agrees with Peter in his account of the outpouring of the Holy Ghost upon the Gentile believers. It is not plainly stated that Paul has reference to this event in his testimony quoted, yet we can see clearly that he does have reference to the experience of sanctification, and that it is identical with that of all believers, being a specific work of the Holy Ghost.

Experiences of the Brethren at Samaria

"Then Philip went down to the city of Samaria, and preached Christ unto them. But when they believed Philip preaching the things concerning the kingdom of God, and the name of Jesus Christ, they were baptized, both men and women."--Acts 8:5, 12. About three years prior to this time there was a greater One than Philip at Samaria preaching the words of life, and many more than the woman at the well believed, and they said to the woman, "Now we believe, not because of thy saying: for we have heard him ourselves, and know that this is indeed the Christ, the Saviour of the world."--John 4:42. This was an effectual introduction of the gospel, and when Philip went to that city he found much good soil for the precious word in the name of Jesus Christ. There is no room for doubt as to the acceptable condition of these converts. They believed in the name of Jesus and were baptized. Some had doubtless remained firm believers since Jesus' visit to that city; others believed through the preaching of Philip. Certainly they were justified by faith in the name of Jesus, but like the disciples before Pentecost they were not yet sanctified, and when the apostles at Jerusalem heard of this work of grace at Samaria they sent down Peter and John, "who when they were come down, prayed for them, that they might receive the Holy Ghost: (For as yet he was fallen upon none of them: only they were baptized in the name of the Lord Jesus) then laid they their hands on them, and they received the Holy Ghost."--Acts 8:15-17.

How clearly the inspired record here proves the second work of grace, and how beautifully this event harmonizes with the others relative to the outpouring of the Holy Spirit. And then, how glorious to have an experience like it in our own hearts. Praise God for this glorious, vivid, and living reality which by its divine power pales every theory into utter obscurity.

CHAPTER III.

Consecration and Dedication

"I beseech you therefore, brethren, by the mercies of God, that ye present your bodies a living sacrifice, holy, acceptable unto God, which is your reasonable service. And be not conformed to this world: but be ye transformed by the renewing of your mind, that ye may prove what is that good, and acceptable, and perfect, will of God."--Romans 12:1, 2.

In this chapter we will notice the scriptures upon the theme of consecration and dedication--the important step necessary on the part of the justified believer, before he can enter into this blessed grace of entire sanctification.

We find that in the old dispensation everything that was to be employed in the service of God necessarily had to be consecrated. In the tabernacle and temple service every vessel and article of furniture, even the smallest spoon, the tongs, and snuffers, together with the building itself, and all the priests and their garments, were consecrated wholly unto God, to be used for no other purpose than divine service. This setting apart for holy service was the Old Testament sanctification. The setting apart of these things, together with the ceremonial application of what God had ordained to be used in this dedication, was acceptable in his sight.

This consecration in the old dispensation is but a shadow of the new. It was God's own way of sanctification--making things holy unto himself. The mere declaration on the part of Moses, in the consecration of these things, that they were now holy, would not have been sufficient without the careful observance of the application of the blood of animals and the holy anointing oil, which were typical of the blood of Jesus and the Holy Spirit. Some of the articles of the tabernacles and temple were sanctified simply by a setting apart and sprinkling with oil (Lev. 8:10), while others required the application of oil and blood. Lev. 8:11, 15. In the consecration of Aaron and his sons the anointing oil and the blood were applied. Without this they would not have been sanctified. Lev. 8:30. The apostle speaks of this in his letter to the Hebrews-- "For if the blood of bulls and of goats, and the ashes of a heifer sprinkling the unclean, sanctifieth to the purifying of the flesh: how much more shall the blood of Christ, who through the eternal Spirit offered himself without spot to God, purge your conscience from dead works to serve the living God?"--Heb. 9:13.

The importance of an exclusive dedication to the service of God should impress our minds with deep solemnity. Anything held back from such a dedication would most certainly have been rejected in the old dispensation, and truly it is the same in the new. Many professing to follow Jesus into a thorough consecration, are at heart disposed to keep back some treasured idol. Many have doubtless made a profession of sanctification, and yet have never made a definite consecration. Such are deceived, and never know the joys of this glorious experience. The cleansing blood and the Holy Spirit will never be applied to the heart that is not absolutely consecrated.

It is both scriptural and logical that we present our bodies a living sacrifice, not only for service but for actual sacrifice in a definite and absolute consecration. We have no bad things to present to the Lord in this consecration; for we are not sinners. We would not be proper candidates for sanctification if we were clinging to anything sinful. Everything sinful must be forsaken and denounced by the guilty sinner when he comes to God for pardon. Otherwise he would never be forgiven of his sins. The world, the flesh, and the devil are forsaken in true repentance. "Denying ungodliness and worldly lusts, we should live soberly, righteously, and godly, in this present world." Therefore all sinful things are laid aside forever in repentance. This is the Bible signification of repentance: To give up all sinful things. But the Bible signification of consecration is to present to Jesus all the sacred treasures of our hearts--give up all our good things.

* * * * *

No sinner can make a definite Bible consecration; for he has no good things to bring to God. He is guilty and condemned in the sight of God. It is the justified believer who has learned by experience that his inward spiritual condition is not yet satisfactory. It may have been for a time; but he sooner or later becomes aware that there is a deeper work of grace needed. He doubts not that he is justified, but knows that something more must be wrought within. Through the ministry of the word of God and the blessed guidance of the Holy Spirit, he is soon taught that a definite consecration must be made as one of the Bible conditions for sanctification. Now comes the searching and far-reaching question: Are you willing to make this consecration? This means everything to the soul. All the sacred God-given treasures around which the heart's affections have so closely entwined, and which have become a part of the very life itself, are now required to be yielded up to Jesus as a voluntary offering. There is no danger that anything will be forgotten; for the heart-searching eye of God will reveal every hidden treasure, and make known the depths of meaning to the soul, which will be astounded to know as never before how much it means to lay all of itself and sacred treasures at the feet of Jesus. There comes an inward struggle, perhaps. The heart's affections tighten around the sacred objects of its love, until they seem dearer than ever before; but while this is being done there comes a sadness stealing over the soul; for whereas these objects seem so sacred and precious, there is a consciousness within that Jesus is slighted. The affections are divided between Jesus and these treasures. He asks the question, "Lovest thou me more than these?" You can answer, "Yes, Lord; thou knowest that I love thee." But must I give up these treasures, these sacred things of my heart for thee? Can not I have both them and thee? This is where death must set in. Thank God, it is the death-route, the only road to this glorious Canaan of soul-rest.

It soon becomes a significant fact thoroughly understood that Jesus requires the undivided heart and every affection. You cannot refuse him. He has done too much for you. He suffered without the gate that he might sanctify you with his own blood. He gave himself for the church that he might sanctify and cleanse it; and now how can you withhold anything from him? He has a just right to all your affections. He gave his all for you, and now it is right that you should give your all for him. He sacrificed his life for you; now you are brought to the sacrifice of your life for him--a living sacrifice. You see that this claim is right and just. It is a reasonable requirement on his part; a "reasonable service" on your part.

But, dear reader, the question must be answered. Are you going to yield? You may answer, Yes; but the Lord requires you to do so at once. Usually when the soul is brought face to face with this consecration and begins to become willing to yield up its treasures, it lets go the easiest ones first, and as one by one they are counted over to the Lord there comes a final struggle; the dearest one of all is now before you. The emotions of the heart begin to deepen as the affections cling to this treasure. Everything has now centered upon this one object. It is to be sacrificed for Jesus or he must be sacrificed for it. Which will it be? It must be Jesus only. Much reasoning may arise upon this important matter, but all is vain. There must be the yielding. You must say from the depths of your soul, "Thy will be done." You have often said this before, but it never meant nearly what it does now. You truly feel the agonies of death. Were you to be laid on your death-bed or in your coffin, there would be no greater separation from everything of this earth than this. No loved one can now go with you. No treasure can be kept as your own. The lone, dark vale must be crossed. No sympathy of friend can follow you. Everything must be left behind. Dear reader, this is a critical moment. The destiny of your soul is hanging upon a single thread. You are swinging out over the deep precipice--clinging, clinging, clinging. Jesus demands that you let go and drop completely into his will. You desire to do this, but your soul shrinks. It seems so dark below. Many a one has here taken counsel with his own soul and decided to swing back upon the side of self, thereby losing incalculable wealth, and missing this glorious soul-rest which "remaineth therefore ... for the people of God." O dear soul, do not fail to labor to enter in! Let the death struggle continue until it has completed its work--until you have truly ceased from your own works. The floodgates of heaven are ready to open and fill you with such glory that it will cause this old world to fade out of sight; but not until you can cheerfully and willingly let go and say to Jesus, "Thy will be done." Your Pentecost is just in reach. Will you have it, or will you not?

In the dedication of the tabernacle we have a beautiful type of the dedication of ourselves to this "reasonable service" of God. The erection of the tabernacle, the placing of all the furniture, and the arrangement of the entire structure had to be made in every respect "according to the pattern" shown to Moses on the mount. In the completion of all the work, we read in Ex. 40 that it was now all done "as the Lord commanded Moses." He might have thought it did not matter much about some of these things, and that the Lord would not require every small thing to be done according to the pattern; but no matter what he might have thought, he knew that obedience to every requirement of the Lord was his only safety; so he made everything according to the pattern. In verse 33 the record says, "So Moses finished the work."

Dear soul, can this be said of you? Have you finished the work? Have you ceased from your own works? You must reach this point in your consecration, so you can realize just as definitely as Moses did, that you have truly finished the work. When this was the condition in the dedication of the tabernacle, "a cloud covered the tent of the congregation, and the glory of the Lord filled the tabernacle. And Moses was not able to enter into the tent of the congregation, because the cloud abode thereon, and the glory of the Lord filled the tabernacle." V. 34. When Moses had finished the work and the dedication was complete, the glory of the Lord came into the tabernacle. So it is with the consecrated heart; the glory of the Lord will fill it.

In the dedication of the temple we also have a type of this Pentecostal experience. "Solomon, and all the congregation of Israel that were assembled unto him before the ark, sacrificed sheep and oxen, which could not be told nor numbered for multitude."--2 Chron. 5:6. See the sacrifice unto the Lord. Nothing was too great; everything was fully yielded up to him without reserve. "And it came to pass, when the priests were come out of the holy place: (for all the priests that were present were sanctified, and did not then wait by course: also the Levites which were the singers, all of them of Asaph, of Heman, of Jeduthun, with their sons and their brethren, being arrayed in white linen having cymbals and psalteries and harps, stood at the east end of the altar, and with them an hundred and twenty priests sounding with trumpets:) it came even to pass, as the trumpeters and singers were as one, to make one sound to be heard in praising and thanking the Lord; and when they lifted up their voice with the trumpets and cymbals and instruments of musick, and praised the Lord, saying, For he is good; for his mercy endureth forever: that then the house was filled with a cloud, even the house of the Lord; so that the priests could not stand to minister by reason of the cloud; for the glory of the Lord had filled the house of God."--2 Chron. 5:11-14. Thus we see that when the sacrifice was complete and everything was in perfect order, the glory of God filled the temple.

This was but a type of the day of Pentecost at Jerusalem. In the type, the glory of the Lord filled the consecrated temple. In the antitype, the consecrated hearts (the temples of the Holy Ghost) were filled with the glory of the Lord. Now this is just what Jesus will do with every consecrated heart today. "He shall baptize you with the Holy Ghost and with fire."--Matt. 3:11. But the consecration must be complete. It is reasonable that Jesus should require us to yield up everything to him. Our hearts cannot be purified until every affection is yielded. He requires this for our own highest good. He wants the supreme right of way so that he can work his own will in our entire being. He wants the absolute control, so that he can get between us and everything. Praise his name! this is for our benefit, which we will plainly see when once we have paid the full price. When his will is completely wrought in us, then he will with himself freely give us all things for our greatest good and his highest glory. Even an hundredfold shall be our delightful portion. But the loss of all things must precede this wonderful increase. An absolute death must precede this abundant life. Then and then only can the Holy Ghost come into and possess the temple. Oh, that every professed believer in Jesus might see the importance of this consecration! The suffering of death is serious indeed; but the unspeakable glory that follows causes the enraptured soul to be astonished at the marvelous gain for so small a loss. The perfect love of Jesus now flows from his heart into the one which has yielded its all to him. The undivided affections now feel the blessedness of perfect unity with him--married indeed to him who is raised from the dead.

CHAPTER IV

The Holy Spirit of Promise

The Holy Spirit was promised through the prophets. "Until the spirit be poured upon us from on high, and the wilderness be a fruitful field, and the fruitful field be counted for a forest. Then judgment shall dwell in the wilderness, and righteousness remain in the fruitful field. And the work of righteousness shall be peace; and the effect of righteousness quietness and assurance forever. And my people shall dwell in a peaceable habitation, and in sure dwellings, and in quiet resting places."--Isa. 32:15-18.

"And I will give them one heart, and I will put a new spirit within you; and I will take the stony heart out of their flesh, and will give them a heart of flesh: that they may walk in my statutes, and keep mine ordinances, and do them: and they shall be my people, and I will be their God."--Ezek. 11:19, 20. "For I will pour water upon him that is thirsty, and floods upon the dry ground: I will pour my spirit upon thy seed, and my blessing upon thine offspring: and they shall spring up as among the grass, as willows by the water courses."--Isa. 44:3, 4.

"Then will I sprinkle clean water upon you, and ye shall be clean: from all your filthiness, and from all your idols, will I cleanse you. A new heart also will I give you, and a new spirit will I put within you: and I will take away the stony heart out of your flesh, and I will give you an heart of flesh. And I will put my spirit within you, and cause you to walk in my statutes, and ye shall keep my judgments, and do them. And ye shall dwell in the land that I gave to your fathers; and ye shall be my people, and I will be your God."--Ezek. 36:25-28.

"And it shall come to pass afterward, that I will pour out my spirit upon all flesh; and your sons and your daughters shall prophesy, your old men shall dream dreams, and your young men shall see visions: and also upon the servants and upon the handmaids in those days will I pour out my spirit."--Joel 2:28, 29.

=Promised through Christ.= "And, behold, I send the promise of my Father upon you: but tarry ye in the city of Jerusalem, until ye be endued with power from on high."--Luke 24:49. "But whosoever drinketh of the water that I shall give him shall never thirst; but the water that I shall give him shall be in him a well of water springing up into everlasting life."--John 4:14. "He that believeth on me, as the scripture hath said, out of his belly shall flow rivers of living water. (But this spake he of the Spirit, which they that believe on him should receive: for the Holy Ghost was not yet given, because that Jesus was not yet glorified.)"--John 7:38, 39.

"If ye love me, keep my commandments. And I will pray the Father, and he shall give you another Comforter, that he may abide with you forever; even the Spirit of truth; whom the world cannot receive, because it seeth him not, neither knoweth him: but ye know him; for he dwelleth with you, and shall be in you. At that day ye shall know that I am in my Father, and ye in me, and I in you. But the Comforter, which is the Holy Ghost, whom the Father will send in my name, he shall teach you all things, and bring all things to your remembrance, whatsoever I have said unto you."--John 14:15-17, 20, 26. "But when the Comforter is come, whom I will send you from the Father, even the Spirit of truth, which proceedeth from the Father, he shall testify of me."--John 15:26.

* * * * *

"Nevertheless I tell you the truth; It is expedient for you that I go away: for if I go not away, the Comforter will not come unto you; but if I depart, I will send him unto you. And when he is come, he will reprove the world of sin, and of righteousness, and of judgment: of sin, because they believe not on me; of righteousness, because I go to my Father, and ye see me no more; of judgment, because the prince of this world is judged. I have yet many things to say unto you, but ye cannot bear them now. Howbeit when he, the Spirit of truth, is come, he will guide you into all truth: for he shall not speak of himself; but whatsoever he shall hear, that shall he speak: and he will show you things to come. He shall glorify me: for he shall receive of mine, and shall show it unto you. All things that the Father hath are mine: therefore said I, that he shall take of mine, and shall show it unto you."--John 16:7-15. "John truly baptized with water; but ye shall be baptized with the Holy Ghost not many days hence."--Acts 1:5.

A Fulfillment of This Promise

"And when the day of Pentecost was fully come, they were all with one accord in one place. And suddenly there came a sound from heaven as of a rushing mighty wind, and it filled all the house where they were sitting. And there appeared unto them cloven tongues like as of fire, and it sat upon each of them. And they were all filled with the Holy Ghost."--Acts 2:1-4.

A Testimony of Its Fulfillment

"But this is that which was spoken by the prophet Joel; and it shall come to pass in the last days, saith God, I will pour out of my Spirit upon all flesh: and your sons and your daughters shall prophesy, and your young men shall see visions, and your old men shall dream dreams: and on my servants and on my handmaidens I will pour out in those days of my Spirit; and they shall prophesy.... This Jesus hath God raised up, whereof we all are witnesses. Therefore being by the right hand of God exalted, and having received of the Father the promise of the Holy Ghost, he hath shed forth this, which ye now see and hear."--Acts 2:16-18, 32, 33.

To Whom Is This Promised?

"Then Peter said unto them, Repent, and be baptized every one of you in the name of Jesus Christ for the remission of sins, and ye shall receive the gift of the Holy Ghost. For the promise is unto you, and to your children, and to all that are afar off, even as many as the Lord our God shall call."--Acts 2:38, 39.

"And we are his witnesses of these things; and so is also the Holy Ghost, whom God hath given to them that obey him."--Acts 5:32. "That the blessing of Abraham might come on the Gentiles through Jesus Christ; that we might receive the promise of the Spirit through faith."--Gal. 3:14.

"That I should be the minister of Jesus Christ to the Gentiles, ministering the gospel of God, that the offering up of the Gentiles might be acceptable, being sanctified by the Holy Ghost."--Rom. 15:16. "But we are bound to give thanks always to God for you, brethren beloved of the Lord, because God hath from the beginning chosen you to salvation through sanctification of the Spirit and belief of the truth."--2 Thess. 2:13.

In a previous chapter we have noticed that the Holy Ghost experience of the apostles and all those of the early church was the same; and we see definitely by the texts just quoted that it is the design of God that all believers receive it. Also we have seen that this Holy Ghost experience is a subsequent one to regeneration, and identical with sanctification. Every young convert who has truly been regenerated, will in due time find that something more needs to be done in his heart before he can fully realize an experience that will correspond with the fulfillment of the many exceeding great and precious promises of the Holy Ghost.

The Scriptures clearly teach us that regeneration is a work of the Holy Spirit. "For by one Spirit are we all baptized into one body."--1 Cor. 12:13. This does not have reference to the Pentecostal baptism, but to the work of the Holy Spirit in regeneration, inducting us into the body of Christ, the church. This is very different from the baptism with the Holy Ghost. In regeneration the Holy Ghost baptizes the believer into Christ; in sanctification Christ baptizes the believer with the Holy Ghost. "He shall baptize you with the Holy Ghost and with fire."--Matt. 3:11.

This latter is the sanctification and Pentecostal experience. Both are spiritual experiences. When reading these wonderful promises by the prophets, we can clearly distinguish the two works of grace foretold.

The birth of the Spirit (John 3:3-8), or that experience which inducts us into Christ, must necessarily precede the experience of sanctification. The Holy Ghost will never come into the temple to abide until he has first gained possession of the same. The heart must first be both justified and fully consecrated before the divine Guest can make it his exclusive and permanent abode. This glorious grace of sanctification does not detract from the marvelous work of justification. Both have their import and place in God's wonderful redemption plan, and stand out distinctly in many of the scriptures; and yet we occasionally hear of some who say of this beautiful doctrine that it is not taught in the word of God. Why such remarks are made is simply because of a misconception of the glorious redemption plan--in some instances it is owing to the perverted doctrines of men, while in others it may be because of a perverted individual experience of justification. To the willing and obedient heart, God will impart knowledge and understanding of his sweet and glorious soul-rest.

Oh, let us praise and magnify the Lord for his wonderful grace that he has so abundantly supplied through repentance toward God and faith toward our Lord Jesus Christ, that he is so willing and ready to remove from our hearts the guilt of all our sins and transgressions, and remember them against us no more forever, and then bestow upon us this blessed inheritance among them which are sanctified by faith that is in Christ Jesus! Would that every justified believer might be kept from all the perverted doctrines of men, so that the heart could receive the knowledge of the pure word of God and become instructed in the doctrine of the Holy Ghost life. The promise of the Father which the resurrected Christ said he would send upon his justified disciples was no more a promise for them than for every justified believer throughout the gospel dispensation. Why then should any of us come short of entering into this blessed covenant of an entire consecration and receiving the fulfillment of the promise? Thank God it is for us and our children and to all that are afar off.

Until the believer reaches this grace, he is not in his normal spiritual condition, and cannot live the Christ-life in a manner that is perfectly satisfactory to his own heart. The great need is a clean heart and the indwelling Holy Spirit, without which there is not the power within at all times to withstand every evil attack of the enemy with perfect victory. Jesus knew this need in his disciples. Their usefulness in the world could not be satisfactory until they received the fulfillment of the promise. They had been useful in his hands and under his personal guidance in the ministry of the gospel of the kingdom. They had already by his help been able to bear fruit, but it was the will of the Father that they should bear more fruit, through the power of the Spirit-filled life; hence they were not to depart from Jerusalem until they were endued with power from on high. "Ye shall receive power after that the Holy Ghost is come upon you." How many of the dear people of God today have never had their Pentecost! Some are out in the world preaching the gospel with no deeper spiritual experience than that of the disciples before they tarried at Jerusalem. Many have mistaken some natural ability for the power of the Holy Ghost. Others have accepted the doctrine of sanctification theoretically--made a formal consecration and claimed the experience, but have never received the Holy Ghost. Dearly beloved brethren and sisters, let us entreat you to tarry and do not depart from your positive death bed consecration, until you are endued with power from on high. It is the will of the Father that you receive the Holy Spirit to possess your being--the consecrated temple--and make your life from this moment a reproduction of the life of Jesus. He is not here now as he was during his earthly ministry, but the Father has designed that the Holy Spirit should dwell in the hearts of consecrated men and women who shall go forth into the world and be witnesses unto Jesus--representatives that will live the Christ-life in this world, so that men may plainly see his character and fruits in us. When Jesus ascended to the throne, he by no means intended that his people should be left comfortless, or deprived of his presence; but rather, he said, "It is expedient for you that I go away."

The "Comforter, which is the Holy Ghost," is the divine executive of Jesus. He was the power and life in Jesus when here in his redemption work, and when he ascended to his throne in heaven the Holy Ghost descended to earth to carry on this glorious redemption work to the end of the world. But he must have human instrumentality through which to work. Where he can find a truly consecrated temple, there he makes his abode, and taking full control of the entire being, performs the perfect will of God through this instrumentality. This is why the apostles were so much more useful after Pentecost than before. They were now fully possessed by the Holy Ghost, and in, through faith in, the name of Jesus were enabled to shake the world. Jesus has left his name here on earth. Through it the Holy Spirit now effects this great redemption. He cannot do this by himself. He cannot "reprove the world of sin, of righteousness, and of judgment," only as he can find consecrated hearts on earth in which to abide. The Spirit-filled lives of the people are the only factors that can be used in the hand of God to produce apostolic results in these perilous days in which we live. This final reformation was unquestionably begun by the power of the

Holy Spirit, and will never be completed by any other power. It is a spiritual work, and only as the glorious doctrine of sanctification is taught and the experience obtained and retained, will the church reach the apostolic plane.

CHAPTER V.

Our Inheritance

"And now, brethren, I commend you to God, and to the word of his grace, which is able to build you up, and give you an inheritance among all them which are sanctified."--Acts 20:32. "And inheritance among them which are sanctified by faith that is in me."--Acts 26:18. "For this is the will of God, even your sanctification."--1 Thess. 4:3.

"That ye be not slothful, but followers of them who through faith and patience inherit the promises. For when God made promise to Abraham, because he could swear by no greater, he sware by himself, saying, Surely blessing I will bless thee, and multiplying I will multiply thee. And so after he had patiently endured, he obtained the promise. For men verily swear by the greater: and an oath for confirmation is to them an end of all strife. Wherein God, willing more abundantly to show unto the heirs of promise the immutability of his counsel, confirmed it by an oath: that by two immutable things, in which it was impossible for God to lie, we might have a strong consolation, who have fled for refuge to lay hold upon the hope set before us: which hope we have as an anchor of the soul, both sure and steadfast, and which entereth into that within the veil."--Heb. 6:12-19.

"But into the second went the high priest alone once every year, not without blood, which he offered for himself, and for the errors of the people: the Holy Ghost this signifying, that the way into the holiest of all was not yet made manifest, while as the first tabernacle was yet standing: which was a figure for the time then present, in which were offered both gifts and sacrifices, that could not make him that did the service perfect, as pertaining to the conscience; which stood only in meats and drinks, and divers washings and carnal ordinances, imposed on them until the time of reformation. But Christ being come an high priest of good things to come, by a greater and more perfect tabernacle, not made with hands, that is to say, not of this building; neither by the blood of goats and calves, but by his own blood he entered in once into the holy place, having obtained eternal redemption for us. For if the blood of bulls and of goats, and the ashes of a heifer sprinkling the unclean, sanctifieth to the purifying of the flesh; how much more shall the blood of Christ, who through the eternal Spirit offered himself without spot to God, purge your conscience from dead works to serve the living God? And for this cause he is the mediator of the new testament, that by means of death, for the redemption of transgressions that were under the first testament, they which are called might receive the promise of eternal inheritance."--Heb. 9:7-15.

"Wherefore when he cometh into the world, he saith, Sacrifice and offering thou wouldest not, but a body hast thou prepared me: ... Above when he said, Sacrifice and offering and burnt offerings and offering for sin thou wouldest not, neither hadst pleasure therein which are offered by the law; then said he, Lo, I come to do thy will, O God. He taketh away the first, that he may establish the second. By the which will we are sanctified through the offering of the body of Jesus Christ once for all ... For by one offering he hath perfected for ever them that are sanctified."--Heb. 10:5, 8-10, 14.

"Husbands, love your wives, even as Christ also loved the church, and gave himself for it; that he might sanctify and cleanse it with the washing of water by the word, that he might present it to himself a glorious church, not having spot, or wrinkle, or any such thing: but that it should be holy and without blemish."--Eph. 5:25-27.

"In whom also we have obtained an inheritance, being predestinated according to the purpose of him who worketh all things after the counsel of his own will: ... in whom ye also trusted, after that ye heard the word of truth, the gospel of your salvation; in whom also after that ye believed ye were sealed with that holy Spirit of promise, which is the earnest of our inheritance until the redemption of the purchased possession, unto the praise of his glory."

"Who gave himself for us, that he might redeem us from all iniquity, and purify unto himself a peculiar people, zealous of good works."--Tit. 2:14. "To perform the mercy promised to our fathers, and to remember his holy covenant; the oath which he sware to our father Abraham, that he would grant unto us, that we being delivered out of the hand of our enemies, might serve him without fear, in holiness and righteousness before him, all the days of our life."--Luke 1:72-75.

"Now to Abraham and his seed were the promises made. He saith not, And to seeds as of many; but as of one, And to thy seed, which is Christ ... For if the inheritance be of the law, it is no more of promise but God gave it to Abraham by promise." "That the blessing of Abraham might come on the Gentiles through Jesus Christ, that we might receive the promise of the Spirit through faith." "And if ye be Christ's, then are ye Abraham's seed, and heirs according to the promise."--Gal. 3:16, 18, 14, 29.

The Abrahamic covenant embraced a twofold nature: the promised seed, and the promised land. Isaac was the literal fulfillment of the promised seed; Canaan, the literal fulfillment of the promised land. These were but the foreshadowing of their great and glorious antitype, Christ and the gospel, which are the spiritual fulfillment of the promises made to Abraham.

"And in thy seed shall all the kindreds of the earth be blessed," which blessing begins in the regenerate heart, is perfected in the inheritance of entire sanctification, and consummated in that inheritance "reserved in heaven for us." That part which is yet reserved in heaven for us will be realized in due time, when this mortal shall put on immortality and the redemption of Christ shall be completed for spirit, soul, and body. We can all rejoice in this "blessed hope" which shall be fully realized when Jesus the resurrected Redeemer shall come again and fashion our dying bodies like unto his glorious body. But the object of this chapter is to point out the scriptures which teach us the blessed truth of the present-tense gospel inheritance, which in the redemption plan is to be realized by the people of God in this gospel dispensation, on this side of the second coming of Christ.

The blessed grace of entire sanctification is scripturally the bequest of God to his people. It is not simply the will of God in the sense that he desires us to have this experience, but it is truly a blood-bought inheritance, provided and willed by our Father through Jesus Christ to every child of God. This blessed experience of regeneration, or the divine birth, inducts us into the family of God, making us a scriptural heir to all the good things of Father's possessions. Father has perfected every necessary provision for every one of his children to come into immediate possession of this inheritance. A will or testament must specify the nature of the inheritance, mention distinctly the names of the heirs, must have the signature of the testator affixed in the presence of witnesses, should appoint an executor, and in every respect it must be perfect or it will not stand legally. Scripturally, this is equally as true. The New Testament is the will, which distinctly specifies the nature of the inheritance of the people of God "among them which are sanctified." The sanctified have entered into their possessions of this Holy Ghost Canaan, and now every regenerated child of God who knows his name is written in Father's family record--the Book of life--soon finds by reading the will that this inheritance is for him. He knows it as he reads and believes, and more and more the Holy Spirit leads him to meet all the spiritual conditions requisite to the coming into possession of this inheritance. He sees also in the will, the signature of the testator. He sees that the Father has authorized Jesus Christ to make this will of force. Legally, a will is not of force until after the death of the testator. Scripturally, this is equally a fact. The child of God sees that it requires the death of the testator to make it possible that he could be sanctified. He reads in the will that Jesus, the testator, suffered without the gate that he might sanctify his people with his own blood and that this is the will of God, even your sanctification.

We see in the will that Father has given every necessary instruction to enable us to meet every condition of entrance into this blessed possession. His word teaches us that as Abraham with faith and patience obtained the promise, so we should profit by his example. God has shown us through his covenant with Abraham that what he promises he is ready and able to fulfill. He has shown his people, who are the heirs of this inheritance, the immutability of his counsel by his word and by his oath, that it is impossible for him to break his word and that we should come to him with perfect confidence that he will do just what he has promised.

There is a remarkable certainty in the fulfillment of this wonderful will. It is as far above any earthly will or testament as the heavens are higher than the earth. In an earthly will made by man, the very incident that makes the will of force also makes it liable to become annulled; for after the death of the testator there frequently is found a defect in the will, also there are instances where the heirs, dissatisfied with their portion of the inheritance, proceed by legal process to annul the entire will and have a new one made according to their own desires. But no such objections can possibly be brought against this divine will.

There are three reasons why it is absolutely beyond the power of man or principality to overthrow this will.

1. It is positively without fault. God had made a will, the old testament, which was defective. The apostle says, "For if that first covenant had been faultless, then should no place have been sought for the second."--Heb. 8:7. In the preceding verse he says, "But now hath he obtained a more excellent ministry, by how much also he is the mediator of a better covenant [testament or will], which was established upon better promises." The blood of those animals in the old covenant was acceptable under that dispensation, but it could not produce the desired effect in sanctification. It could only sanctify to the purifying of the flesh; could not reach the spiritual and moral nature of man; for there was no spiritual nor moral nature in the sacrifice. It was only a sacrifice of animal life; therefore it could only purify the flesh, or animal life, of man (Heb. 9:13) in a ceremonial sense. Therefore, the first will or testament was necessarily defective, and God himself has annulled it. Heb. 8:13. But Father's last will is vastly different. It is complete, perfect, and utterly without fault.

2. It is so divinely and infinitely perfect in its power to sanctify and reach every inmost need of the heart that none of the heirs can possibly become dissatisfied with their individual portion; for this portion is the entire inheritance for each individual heir. It is not divided into certain bounded portions for different heirs, but each is entitled to the entire inheritance, and can come into the full enjoyment of the whole possession without diminishing, in the least degree, the privilege of every heir to enjoy the same. This makes it unspeakably satisfactory. But what yet adds to it in its power to satisfy, is that, the sacrifice which was required to bring this will and testament into force was the precious blood of Christ. The great purpose of God in this judicial sacrifice was that the sins of the world might be forgiven, that we might thus become the sons of God and heirs of this inheritance. But, my dear brother and sister, our Saviour had also another purpose in view in this stupendous sacrifice. He gave himself for the church, that he might sanctify and cleanse it. Eph. 5:25, 26 and Heb. 13:12.

Ah, dear reader, do you not see your inheritance in this? His blood can sanctify wholly our spiritual, moral and physical nature. The blood of the old will had no spiritual nor moral power in it at all; therefore, no wonder it could sanctify only to the purifying of the flesh. But, oh, the matchless, marvelous grace of God to prepare a sacrifice (a body--Heb. 10:5) pure and spotless spiritually, morally, and physically, which blood can cleanse our corresponding nature spiritually, morally, and physically, and reaching every spot of our entire being, make us clean from the least and last remains of sin. In comparing these sacrifices no wonder the apostle asks, "How much more shall the blood of Christ, who through the eternal Spirit offered himself without spot to God, purge your conscience from dead works to serve the living God?" Truly, when we have obtained this inheritance we can sing with the inspired poet

"I have found it, Lord, in thee, An everlasting store, Of comfort, joy, and bliss to me, How can I wish for more?"

Praise God for the cleansing which reaches our inmost soul and saves to the uttermost! It, therefore, readers, is impossible for the heir to become dissatisfied with the inheritance.

3. To make the inheritance doubly certain, we have already seen that God has confirmed it by two immutable things; his word, and his oath; but to add still more to this matter and make it absolutely certain and impossible for any principality or power to overthrow this will, God has appointed Jesus Christ to be executor of his own will. From a human standpoint this would be impossible; for the will could not be of force at all while the testator was alive, and his death would render him incapable of any part in it as an executor. But with God these things are possible; for when the testator died that he might bring this will into force, he could not be holden by the power of death; but arose again from the dead, that he might lead captivity captive and give gifts unto men. Thus he has become the executor of his own will, and now stands ready to bestow upon every heir the full possession of his inheritance.

Dear reader, this is the glorious land of promise of which the land of Canaan was but a type. The children of Israel were the heirs of that land because they were the children of Abraham. We are heirs to this Holy Ghost Canaan because we are the children of God through Christ. This Holy Spirit life can only be obtained through this God-appointed plan. It is the "inheritance among them which are sanctified." God gave it to Abraham by promise, and as his faith grasped hold on the promises he saw beyond the literal seed into the blessings of the gospel of Christ and this glorious Holy Spirit life. Christ has fulfilled these promises which Abraham saw and believed; and now the apostle can truly say in looking over this wonderful plan, that "they which be of faith are blessed with faithful Abraham. That the blessing of Abraham might come on the Gentiles through Jesus Christ; that we might receive the promise of the Spirit through faith."--Gal. 3:9, 14.

CHAPTER VI.

Sanctified by Faith

"But without faith it is impossible to please him: for he that cometh to God must believe that he is, and that he is a rewarder of them that diligently seek him."--Heb. 11:6.

"That they may receive forgiveness of sins, and inheritance among them which are sanctified by faith that is in me."--Acts 26:18.

"Therefore being justified by faith, we have peace with God through our Lord Jesus Christ: by whom also we have access by faith into this grace wherein we stand."--Rom. 5:1, 2.

Faith in the blood of Christ. "Wherefore Jesus also, that he might sanctify the people with his own blood, suffered without the gate."--Heb. 13:12. "But if we walk in the light, as he is in the light, we have fellowship one with another, and the blood of Jesus Christ his Son cleanseth us from all sin."--1 John 1:7.

Dead to sin by faith. "Knowing this, that our old man is crucified with him, that the body of sin might be destroyed, that henceforth we should not serve sin. For he that is dead is freed from sin ... Likewise reckon ye also yourselves to be dead indeed unto sin, but alive unto God through Jesus Christ our Lord."--Rom. 6:6, 7, 11.

Free from sin by faith. "Being then made free from sin, ye became the servants of righteousness ... For as ye have yielded your members servants to uncleanness and to iniquity unto iniquity; even so now yield your members servants to righteousness unto holiness ... But now being made free from sin, and become servants to God, ye have your fruit unto holiness, and the end everlasting life."--Rom. 6:18-22. "Jesus answered them, Verily, verily, I say unto you, Whosoever committeth sin is the servant of sin. And the servant abideth not in the house for ever: but the Son abideth ever. If the Son therefore shall make you free, ye shall be free indeed."--John 8:34-36.

"And ye know that he was manifested to take away our sins; and in him is no sin. Whosoever abideth in him sinneth not: whosoever sinneth hath not seen him, neither known him.... He that committeth sin is of the devil; for the devil sinneth from the beginning. For this purpose the Son of God was manifested, that he might destroy the works of the devil. Whosoever is born of God doth not commit sin; for his seed remaineth in him: and he cannot sin, because he is born of God. In this the children of God are manifest, and the children of the devil."--1 John 3:5-10.

A pure heart by faith. "And God, which knoweth the hearts, bare them witness, giving them the Holy Ghost, even as he did unto us; and put no difference between us and them, purifying their hearts by faith."--Acts 15:8, 9.

We receive the Holy Spirit by faith. "That the blessing of Abraham might come on the Gentiles through Jesus Christ: that we might receive the promise of the Spirit through faith."--Gal. 3:14. "That I should be the minister of Jesus Christ to the Gentiles, ministering the gospel of God, that the offering up of the Gentiles might be acceptable, being sanctified by the Holy Ghost."--Rom. 15:16. "If ye then, being evil [earthly], know how to give good gifts unto your children: how much more shall your heavenly Father give the Holy Spirit to them that ask him?"--Luke 11:13.

Sanctification is a redemption blessing offered to us upon specified conditions. The natural and general blessings of God toward men, such as the sunshine, rain, and all other temporal or earthly blessings, may be received alike by both saint and sinner, who come into conformity with the natural laws by which these natural blessings are governed. Every redemption or spiritual blessing is also governed by divinely fixed laws, which if complied with will invariably bring to us all that is contained in the promise. God is able to bestow upon us these blessings unconditionally if this should be his sovereign will in some individual instances; but according to his redemption plan there is no assurance given to anyone for any of these specified blessings without a strict conformity to divine law. The word of God plainly sets forth the laws upon which these different redemption blessings are based. Repentance and faith are the laws of justification. It is a divinely established fact that God cannot lie. He has forever settled his word in heaven and also upon earth;

therefore, it is impossible that any sinner should comply with the laws of repentance and faith and not be justified. Consecration and faith are the laws of sanctification, which if complied with, must necessarily bring us into this glorious soul-rest.

We have considered the law of consecration as a condition of sanctification in a previous chapter; and from the quoted texts in this chapter we will now briefly consider the law of faith. These laws are definitely fixed, and must as definitely be complied with. A definite consecration and a definite faith will produce a definite experience. One great lack in the church today is a lack of definiteness. The doctrine of sanctification must be more definitely taught by God's anointed ministry, who have themselves definitely met the conditions, both to obtain and retain this definite experience. When it is definitely taught it will consequently be definitely sought and obtained.

In the apostle's commission we distinctly see that we are sanctified by faith. Acts 26:18. We also see that Jesus suffered on the cross that he might sanctify us with his own blood. This points us to the fact that we must have faith in his blood. This grace is purchased for us, and now it is for us to receive it. We also see that he has made provision in this same purchase that we may be kept sanctified. This is upon the simple condition of walking in the light as he is in the light. The result of which is: his blood cleanseth us from all sin. These precious truths will do us no good if we do not believe them. No heart can ever receive the benefits of this inestimable purchase without faith. Faith is the hand that reaches out and takes it. Jesus can do no more than he has done to bring it to us. He holds it out to us, all perfect and complete, and as we meet the conditions of consecration and faith it becomes ours.

The apostle teaches us in Rom. 6:11 to reckon ourselves "dead indeed unto sin." This can be done only by faith. The reckoning of faith is a very simple process; it is just believing God. Abraham believed God, simply reckoned that what God said was true, and then God counted something to Abraham. He counted it to him for righteousness.

This is the divine law of faith. When we believe it is so because God says it, then God makes it so because we believe it. This law applies to all the graces of the gospel alike. It is a sad fact that some professing Christians do not believe we can be sanctified in this life. Now, it is utterly impossible for such people to get it. They do not believe. The blood of Christ cannot sanctify them in this condition. It is not for them at all. It is only for them that believe, and of course no one can believe for it in the scriptural sense without having met the condition of scriptural consecration. Then the scriptural reckoning will bring the scriptural and satisfactory result.

Let us illustrate with a simple mathematical reckoning. In a case of addition we take two numbers and reckon them together before we get the sum. It can never be obtained any other way. The two numbers are entirely distinct and separate from each other until they are reckoned together. It is the reckoning that produces the sum. This is exactly true in the process of faith. The justified believer comes to God for his inheritance of sanctification. He makes the absolute and definite consecration. He sees that the blood of Jesus has been shed that he may be sanctified. This is Jesus' part. The consecration is the believer's part. There are the two separate parts which, if they are not reckoned together, will never produce the result. We might say that we have now made the consecration, and can do no more. This would be a mistake, we can do more: we have not yet done the reckoning. We can take the two parts, the blood of Jesus and our consecration, and by faith add them together, and according to the immutable law of God, which is the law of faith, the sum of the reckoning is, our sanctification. This is the scriptural method of obtaining this experience; and as we from henceforth reckon ourselves dead indeed unto sin upon the condition of an absolute, unbroken consecration, we may rest assured that the blood of Jesus keeps us cleansed from all sin. The fact that some one may say he does not believe we can be kept free from sin, by no means affects this divine law. It is as true as heaven, despite all the unbelief of men. Oh, the power of the sin-cleansing blood! Can we not say with deep, heartfelt reality,

"Hallelujah for the cleansing; It has reached my inmost soul"?

Truly it is the sweet soul-rest, the heavenly Canaan of the soul, which is the inheritance of the people of God.

The apostle Peter, in his testimony of the inwrought grace of God at Pentecost, speaks of this law of faith, which effected in him and his brethren at Jerusalem, as well as the household of Cornelius upon the event of their induction into this glorious grace, the experience of heart purity, "and put no difference between us and them, purifying their hearts by faith." This is one phase of sanctification, and according to the testimony of Peter, was a part of the pentecostal experience. The other phase of it is, in the previous verse of this testimony, "giving them the Holy Ghost, even as he did unto us." This is explained by the apostle Paul. "That we might receive the promise of the Spirit through faith."--Gal. 3:14. Now if we turn to Rom. 15:16, again we see that we are "sanctified by the Holy Ghost." Certainly it could not be made more plain than these scriptures set it forth. We receive the pure heart and the Holy Spirit by faith, which experience is scripturally termed sanctification; therefore, we can understand the language of Jesus in that part of the commission of the apostle already quoted: "and inheritance among them which are sanctified by faith that is in me."

Dear brother and sister, let us magnify God and the name of Jesus for our inheritance, and if there should be one reader who has not yet entered into this promised land, let us go over at once and possess it.

We see a beautiful example of faith in the experience of the children of Abraham crossing the Jordan to enter into their literal inheritance. The priests that bore the ark, which went before the people, were to be the first to go down into the stream, which, God had said, should be divided, and the people should go over into their inheritance. As they came down to the river, their feet were dipped into the stream before the waters parted. God had promised it. They believed it and obeyed accordingly, and God fulfilled his promise; the waters were parted, and they all passed over. How different this was from those who, forty years previous to this event had been brought by the hand of God to

Kadesh Barnea, who had all the promises of God in their favor, that he would cause them to go in and possess the land. But because of unbelief they were sent back into the wilderness, to wander and die. This literal Canaan was their promised land, their land of rest, their very own; God had promised Abraham that it should be possessed by his seed. But these forfeited it because of unbelief. This was the type of this spiritual inheritance of sanctification, our land of rest, our very own, which we, the spiritual seed of Abraham through faith in Christ, are to go into and possess.

The apostle gives us some wholesome admonition upon the importance of seeking to enter in. "Take heed, brethren, lest there be in any of you an evil heart of unbelief, in departing from the living God."--Heb. 3:4. An evil heart of unbelief will most certainly cause us to lose our inheritance. We are made partakers of it only by faith. As certainly as the unbelief of literal children of Abraham caused them to be rejected and disinherited, so will unbelief cause the same sad result in losing the spiritual inheritance. They provoked God with their unbelief, and he who had sworn to Abraham that his seed should possess Canaan, now sware that these unbelieving ones should not enter in. They could not enter in because of unbelief. God's word was not broken, however; for he brought into this land those of the children who, their unbelieving fathers said, would become a prey to the inhabitants of the land. And, what still keeps God's word from being broken is, that he has opened to us this glorious spiritual land, and tells us to go over and possess it. Dear brother, are you at Kadesh Barnea today, and afraid of the giants? God has given the land to us. The message of reproof comes to you with this solemn and important question, "How long are ye slack to go to possess the land which the Lord God of your fathers hath given you?"

This gospel of sanctification is preached to us today as the gospel of literal Canaan was preached to those descendants of Abraham in that day. It did not profit them, not being mixed with faith in them that heard it. The apostle says, "We which have believed do enter into rest," but more must enter in. God's promise to Abraham must yet be more completely fulfilled. The question is simply left with us, Will we enter in or will we not? If we will not, then the inheritance will be given to others, and we will lose the blessed soul-rest that is provided in this redemption for the people of God. In his exhortation to us, the apostle says "Let us labor therefore to enter into that rest, lest any man fall after the same example of unbelief."

"Oh, this blessed holy rest, On my Jesus' loving breast. Oh, the sweetness and completeness Of perfected holiness."

CHAPTER VII

The Subtraction Process

The baptism with the Holy Ghost and fire, the entering into the heavenly inheritance of Canaan, and the possession of the land, and all the blessings that follow are unmistakably a process of addition to the already blessed experience of the justified soul. This addition is scripturally termed "sanctification." No mortal language can ever express how much of an addition it is; but there must necessarily precede this marvelous grace, a definite and absolute subtraction, a loss of all things for the excellency of Christ, a complete self-abnegation, which has been mentioned in a previous chapter upon consecration. Until this absolute loss of all things has been truly experienced, there cannot be obtained the gain of this additional experience. We cannot lay hold of the promised inheritance until we completely let go of everything else that has been called our own.

There is, within our spiritual, moral, and physical nature, a depravity, "our old man," which must be extracted before we can possess the purity of heart so plainly taught in the word of God. This depravity is so deeply embedded in, and interwoven into, our affections and nature, that, like a closely fitting garment, it seems a part of us; and were it not for the plain teachings of the word of God, and the power of the all-cleansing blood of Christ which can reach the inmost center of our nature, purging out all unnatural tendencies and unholy tempers, the justified believer might conclude that this inborn depravity must be permitted to exist and remain with us all through life. But thank God! there is a remedy in this great redemption plan. The heart can be purified and become a holy temple for the indwelling of the Holy Ghost. This depends upon the plainly specified conditions taught in the word of God. He will prepare the temple for his abode if we but furnish him an absolute consecration of the temple. This is our part in this preparatory stage of the work of sanctification. In order that he may purify our nature, we must yield up to him everything that is to be purified. This process involves the loss of all things; for when the heart is thus yielded, everything that it clings to is also yielded, and then, and only then, can the blood of Christ be applied for a perfect cleansing. This is where the subtraction work is effected, where every vestige of depravity is removed from the heart; because it has for this purpose yielded to Jesus. The following scripture sets forth this experience.

* * * * *

"Knowing this, that our old man is crucified with him, that the body of sin might be destroyed, that henceforth we should not serve sin."--Rom. 6:6. It cannot be improved upon nor cultivated. It is sinful in nature, and must be dealt with according to the redemption law of crucifixion. It is condemned and must die. It is utterly worthless to God, and harmful to man; therefore, it must die. It clings to life with remarkable tenacity, and it is not within the power of man alone to put it to death. It has so entwined itself into our affections that they and each of their objects must be absolutely yielded up to death, even the most sacred treasures of the heart; so that the true work of purity may be perfectly wrought within us. To simply yield up our old man for his destruction would be but a pleasant sacrifice; for every justified believer who has obtained the knowledge of this enemy within becomes anxious for his destruction. It is not the yielding up of our old man, therefore, that seems such a loss to us; but when we see that our whole being, spirit, soul, and body, with every affection and its object, must be yielded up and truly laid upon the altar, we realize the subtraction process of sanctification--the loss of all things. Our old man cannot be crucified until everything is thus first yielded up. As long as any one object of our affection is withheld, the consecration is incomplete and the affections can not be purified from this depravity; hence the necessity of an absolute yielding up of everything, to obtain the excellency of this heavenly grace. In this condition we can assuredly experience the meaning of the words: "Knowing this, that our old man is crucified with him, that the body of sin might be destroyed." Thank God! this is a present-tense experience for everyone who is willing to be conformed to the perfect will of God. In this condition, Jesus can have the perfect right of way within, and work in us that which is well-pleasing in his sight.

Some one might wonder if we are never permitted in this truly consecrated condition, to set our affections upon anything in this world, or, if we can possess anything as our own, if all must be yielded up and laid upon the altar. If our affections and every object of the same are yielded to Jesus, then we certainly cannot have them placed upon anything else. This is one of the grand provisions of his grace. Jesus now gets between us and every object of our affections. He not only has our affections, but he has the objects of our affections. In the consciousness of this loss to us we also become conscious of the loss of our old, depraved nature, and the gain of a glorious, heavenly purity which we before did not possess. But above all things, we become conscious of the fact that Jesus has become enthroned within our hearts, and now has full control of our entire being. In him we possess all things. He gives us back, with himself, everything that is good for us: father, mother, brother, sister, and every God-given blessing that we had yielded up to him. But they do not seem to us now like they did before. There is something between us and them. What is it? It is Jesus! This makes every blessing so much more precious to us now. A sacredness exists between us and our loved ones which we never realized before. They now get our love only as they get it through Jesus, for he is between us and them. Praise God for this precious experience! We gave everything, our all, for him. He purified our hearts and now gives everything, his all, to us. Without the subtraction of our all, first, we cannot obtain the addition, his all. Thus, after all, we lose nothing but the depravity of our nature, which loss, of course, involves the loss of all things for the time being, but means the gain of all things in the fullness of Christ.

The apostle Paul expresses this crucifixion in his testimony in Gal. 2:20 "I am crucified with Christ: nevertheless I live; yet not I, but Christ liveth in me: and the life which I now live in the flesh I live by the faith of the Son of God, who loved me, and gave himself for me." There was something of the apostle that was crucified. It was the same as he speaks of in Rom. 6:6, "our old man." That depraved, carnal self, the proud, haughty Pharisee, the great Saul of Tarsus who considered himself of such importance among men. This was the =I= that was crucified; but there was an =I= who still lived. This was the humble, sanctified Paul, the servant of Jesus Christ, who now considered himself less than the least of all saints, and not worthy to be called an apostle. What a contrast between the two =I='s. The one, the big =I=; the other, the little =I=. They are exactly of opposite natures. The one was Paul's "old man," the other his humble individual self. Jesus and the big I cannot rule together in the same heart.

How many there are today who have not reached the death experience. They have had their sins forgiven and realize that they are the children of God; but they cannot say that they are crucified with Christ, in the sense of the actual death of their old man. How many there are who are conscious of this inward foe, and yet are taught that it can never become dislodged from their nature and crucified. Praise God! he has provided a remedy in the blood of Christ. By faith in this blood the consecrated believer can receive the cleansing. The depraved nature is crucified, and Christ now takes supreme control of the holy temple.

The language of the apostle in Gal. 6:14 also expresses the same experience: "But God forbid that I should glory, save in the cross of our Lord Jesus Christ, by whom the world is crucified unto me, and I unto the world." The blood of the cross has destroyed that inward nature which was the point of contact with the world. As long as this exists within, the world has a strong claim upon us, which, so long as it exists within us, will assert its nature, and, if permitted, will communicate with the world, and cause defeat in our Christian life, so that we cannot conscientiously say we are dead to the world: for there is something within us yet that is actually alive in this respect. This is the point of inward contact with the world, which, when brought into crucifixion, changes our inward condition and enables us to truly say with the apostle, that the world is crucified unto us and we unto the world, by the blood of the cross of Christ, and the life we now live in this mortal body, which is the temple of the Holy Ghost, we live by the faith of the Son of God, who has all power to keep us in the divine law of the Spirit of life in Christ Jesus, which makes and keeps us free from the law of sin and death.

In Matt. 15:13 we have this same doctrine of cleansing expressed in the words of Jesus: "Every plant, which my heavenly Father hath not planted, shall be rooted up." While it is true that Jesus was speaking of the doctrines of the Pharisees in this instance, we can see beyond the simple doctrines and traditions of men, which are but the outgrowth of this root of depravity which our heavenly Father never planted in the nature of man. The depraved heart is the fertile soil which spontaneously grows all these evil things which Jesus mentions in this parable. The root is there, and so long as it remains, there cannot be a satisfactory Christian life. But the heavenly decree has been uttered by the Redeemer himself, that this plant shall be rooted up, which rooting up can be testified to by thousands of blood-washed saints today. Many plain scriptures teach us that this experience of heart purity was a recognized fact in the apostolic days. Jesus taught that it was attainable and told of its blessings when in Matt. 5:8 he speaks of the pure in heart. John writes: "And every man that hath this hope in him purifieth himself, even as he is pure." Paul says that "the end of the commandment is charity out of a pure heart" (1 Tim. 1:5), and in the same letter he writes: "Holding the mystery of the faith in a pure conscience."--Chap. 3:9. Also in Chap. 4:12, he writes: "Let no man despise thy youth: but be thou an example of the believers, in word, in conversation, in charity, in spirit, in faith, in purity." In Chap. 5:22, he says, "Keep thyself pure." In 2 Tim. 2:22 we are taught that many of the saints had this experience of cleansing: "Flee also youthful lusts; but follow righteousness, faith, charity, peace, with them that call on the Lord out of a pure heart."

The prophet Malachi saw the glorious fullness of this gospel salvation as he beheld and spake by the Spirit: "And he shall sit as a refiner and purifier of silver and he shall purify the sons of Levi, and purge them as gold and silver, that they may offer unto the Lord an offering in righteousness."--Mal. 3:3.

All these plain texts set forth the doctrines of cleansing beyond question. Then when Peter takes the witness-stand (Acts 15:9) and testifies that he and all the one hundred twenty at Pentecost, and afterward the household of Cornelius, received the cleansing at the time of the outpouring upon them of the Holy Spirit, we must acknowledge that God certainly is no respecter of persons, and has the same measure of grace for his people in this evening time of the gospel day. Praise his holy name! Let us magnify and exalt the power of the all-cleansing blood, for it can reach beyond the inmost depths of our fallen nature and wash us whiter than snow. "For if the blood of bulls and of goats, and the ashes of a heifer, sprinkling the unclean, sanctifieth to the purifying of the flesh: how much more shall the blood of Christ, who through the eternal Spirit offered himself without spot to God, purge your conscience from dead works to serve the living God?"--

"Oh, now I see the cleansing wave, That fountain deep and wide; Jesus, my Lord, mighty to save, Points to his wounded side.

"The cleansing stream, I see, I see, I plunge, and oh, it cleanseth me Oh, praise the Lord, it cleanseth me! It cleanseth me, yes, cleanseth me."

CHAPTER VIII

Christian Perfection

Definition of =perfection=: Unblemished, blameless, pure.

We are commanded to be perfect. "Be ye therefore perfect, even as your Father which is in heaven is perfect."--Matt. 5:48. "For we are glad, when we are weak, and ye are strong: and this also we wish, even your perfection. Finally, brethren, farewell. Be perfect, be of good comfort, be of one mind, live in peace; and the God of love and peace shall be with you."--2 Cor. 13:9,

11. "Therefore leaving the principles of the doctrine of Christ, let us go on unto perfection."--Heb. 6:1.

We must be perfect in love. "Thou shalt love the Lord thy God with all thy heart, and with all thy soul, and with all thy strength, and with all thy mind; and thy neighbor as thyself."--Luke 10:27. "And above all these things put on charity, which is the bond of perfectness."--Col. 3:14. "But whoso keepeth his word, in him verily is the love of God perfected: hereby know we that we are in him."--1 John 2:5. "If we love one another, God dwelleth in us, and his love is perfected in us.... Herein is our love made perfect, that we may have boldness in the day of judgment: because as he is, so are we in this world."--1 John 4:12, 17.

Perfect in unity. "For both he that sanctifieth and they who are sanctified are all of one: for which cause he is not ashamed to call them brethren."--Heb. 2:11. "And for their sakes I sanctify myself, that they also might be sanctified through the truth. Neither pray I for these alone, but for them also which shall believe on me through their word: that they all may be one; as thou, Father, art in me, and I in thee, that they also may be one in us: that the world may believe that thou hast sent me. And the glory which thou gavest me I have given them; that they may be one, even as we are one: I in them, and thou in me, that they may be made perfect in one; and that the world may know that thou hast sent me, and hast loved them, as thou hast loved me."--John 17:19-23.

Perfect in Christ. "Whom we preach, warning every man, and teaching every man in all wisdom; that we may present every man perfect in Christ Jesus." "And ye are complete in him, which is the head of all principality and power." "Epaphras, who is one of you, a servant of Christ, saluteth you, always laboring fervently for you in prayers, that ye may stand perfect and complete in all the will of God."--Col. 1:28; 2:10; 4:12.

Perfect in purity. "Beloved, now are we the sons of God, and it doth not yet appear what we shall be: but we know that, when he shall appear, we shall be like him; for we shall see him as he is. And every man that hath this hope in him purifieth himself even as he is pure."--1 John 3:2, 3. "Having therefore these promises, dearly beloved, let us cleanse ourselves from all filthiness of the flesh and spirit, perfecting holiness in the fear of God."--2 Cor. 7:1. "And the Lord make you to increase and abound in love one toward another, and toward all men, even as we do toward you: to the end he may stablish your hearts unblameable in holiness before God, even our Father, at the coming of our Lord Jesus Christ with all his saints."--1 Thess. 3:12, 13.

This perfection is attainable. "Till we all come in the unity of the faith, and of the knowledge of the Son of God, unto a perfect man, unto the measure of the stature of the fulness of Christ."--Eph. 4:13. "Let us therefore, as many as be perfect, be thus minded: and if in anything ye be otherwise minded, God shall reveal even this unto you."--Phil. 3:15. "For by one offering he hath perfected forever them that are sanctified."--Heb. 10:14. "For the law made nothing perfect, but the bringing in of a better hope did; by the which we draw nigh unto God."--Heb. 7:19. "Which was a figure for the time then present, in which were offered both gifts and sacrifices, that could not make him that did the service perfect, as pertaining to the conscience."--Heb. 9:9.

A perfection not attainable in this life. "Not as though I had already attained, either were already perfect: but I follow after, if that I may apprehend that for which also I am apprehended of Christ Jesus."

Christian perfection is not maturity in wisdom, grace, or knowledge. "Ye therefore, beloved, seeing ye know these things before, beware lest ye also, being led away with the error of the wicked, fall from your own steadfastness. But grow in grace, and in the knowledge of our Lord and Saviour Jesus Christ."--2 Pet. 3:17, 18.

Christian perfection is looked upon by some as an impossibility in this life; but when we turn to the word of God and see the many plain texts upon the subject, it must become evident to every candid mind that it is in the plan of redemption that every child of God should attain to it. It would not be according to the nature of divine grace to require of us anything we could not do. No reasonable earthly parent would demand an impossibility of a child, and it is certain our heavenly Father would not command us to be "perfect even as he is perfect" unless he has provided abundant grace to bring us up to this blessed experience. According to our own power or ability we could never reach such an exalted plane, for it is not within the power of man to change his depraved nature, and every self-effort to reach a state of perfection is but vain. But God is able to make all grace abound and as an All-wise Father he has made it possible that we should be perfect.

From the scriptures quoted we can plainly see that the perfection required of us is reasonable and just. Had he commanded us to be perfect in knowledge, wisdom, judgment, or in anything else in an absolute sense, we would be forced to the conclusion that God has either required an impossibility of us or it is not for us to attain in this life and therefore belongs only to the resurrected state. But we can clearly see the nature of his requirements and that they are all within the limits of his grace toward us in this life.

When Jesus commanded us to be perfect (Matt. 5:48) we can quite easily comprehend his meaning when we notice in the few preceding verses that we should be perfect in love, even to the extent that we shall love our enemies, that we may indeed be the children of our Father which is in heaven. The children of this world love those that love them. It is an easy matter and quite natural to do this. But to love our enemies is very contrary to the depraved nature; unless there has been the cleansing wrought within, there will be some inward consciousness of hatred toward those who despitefully use and persecute us. The high standard of righteousness which Jesus teaches here and throughout this chapter is the standard of sanctification. The love of God must be perfected in us, which destroys every element of the old nature, of which hatred is a prominent characteristic.

The first and great commandment, both of the old and new dispensation, "Thou shalt love the Lord thy God with all thy heart," etc., is also a standard too high to be attained perfectly without the experience of entire sanctification.

This commandment was given during the old dispensation; but it was not possible then that it could be kept perfectly, for there was no provision then made to destroy the power of, and cleanse the heart from, inbred depravity. The blood of those sacrifices could do no more than sanctify "to the purifying of the flesh." The inward condition of the heart could not be changed. Thus we see clearly that this commandment could not be kept in the New Testament sense of perfect love. Now, the blood of Jesus, which he shed on the cross that he might sanctify and cleanse our hearts, can make us holy. When the heart has realized the power of this cleansing and the love of God "shed abroad in our hearts by the Holy Ghost," we can in deed and in truth love the Lord our God with all our heart, soul, mind, and strength. Praise God for his wonderful love to us! He furnishes the love with which to love him. If we but give him our hearts he will furnish all the rest. He wants an empty, clean vessel into which to pour out his love, that it may be manifested in this dark and sinful world.

Oh, that every child of God could see the imperative need of an absolute consecration and then cheerfully and voluntarily meet the conditions of the same, so that God could fill each heart with love, and cause each one to know what it means to love God with all our heart. As long as our affections are divided between God and anything else, our love is not perfect and until the regenerate heart has made the scriptural consecration, there will be a divided condition of the affections. The obedient regenerate heart dwells in God, and thus is taught of God the necessity of the perfect consecration, which, when fully complied with, enables the perfect cleansing to become effected. The apostle John says, "Herein is our love made perfect," and "his love is perfected in us."

No one can ever be fully satisfied in this redemption life until this second work of grace is accomplished in the heart. Justification brings us into the blessed kingdom of God's love. Sanctification perfects his love in us. This second grace enables us to realize not only the meaning of perfect love, but we also comprehend the glorious fact that God has wrought in us perfect purity and holiness. This implies our being perfect in God's will, and because we have yielded our will completely to him. Every disposition of our will which sought its own way is now in perfect conformity with his and as Jesus could say in Gethsemane, "Thy will be done," which meant death on Calvary to him, so we have said the same to God with a vivid consciousness that once for all it meant death to us. It has required the perfect will of Jesus to obtain this grace of sanctification for us, and it now requires our perfect will to receive it from him. Here is where we can stand perfect and complete in all the will of God. Another beautiful characteristic of sanctification is perfect unity. One of the most striking features of the religious world today is division among those who profess to believe in and follow Christ. There is no greater evil existing than this. Men have made creeds and sects and have persuaded the people to join them, until the disgusting spectacle of division is seen everywhere, and the non-professing world is amazed at the sickening sight. Hireling preachers are pleading for their respective denominations, and while many honest children of God are dissatisfied with this sad state of affairs, they are taught from the pulpit that God has made these divisions and it is the duty of every Christian to join and support them. But such is not the will of God; he has designed that his people should all be one, and in his prayer Jesus expresses the extent of this unity. "That they all may be one; as thou, Father, art in me, and I in thee, that they also may be one in us." This certainly implies a wonderful and perfect unity. Many sect advocates cry, "Impossible, impossible; God's people cannot be one." But the whole theme of Jesus' prayer is unity. As we carefully read this prayer we can readily perceive the divine method to effect this unity. It is plain and simple: "Sanctify them through thy truth: thy word is truth.... Neither pray I for these alone, but for them also which shall believe on me through their word; that they all may be one." Then in Heb. 2:11 we see again that this is God's plan--"For both he that sanctifieth and they who are sanctified are all of one."

This grace not only brings us into a perfect inward unity with Jesus himself, but it just as truly brings us all into a perfect inward unity with each other. Divisions, sects, and factions are productions of the flesh (Gal. 5:19-21) and not of the Spirit. Sanctification destroys all the works of the flesh and extracts the very root itself and renders divisions impossible. Every sect yoke is destroyed because of the anointing. Isa. 10:27. It is the work of the Holy Spirit to effect this unity in us with God and with each other. Every human effort to accomplish this must necessarily end in failure. There are many efforts today to effect a union among Christians, but union is not scriptural unity. Union of sects is far from the scriptural unity of believers. A union consists upon a human basis and may consist of a union of sects, or a union of individuals, without any conditions of spirituality whatever. Each individual or body retaining its distinctive and separate division. Scriptural unity is based upon the inner-wrought grace of sanctification, where everything non-spiritual is entirely destroyed and the Holy Spirit has the right of way in every respect according to the perfect will of God.

It is only as we are thus perfected in this grace that the prayer of Jesus will be fully answered and his people lose every vestige of division. No sanctified heart can remain loyal to anything that separates the people of God. All sect holiness is below the Bible standard, for it upholds that which sanctification destroys. This is a far-reaching assertion, but in the light of God's word it is true. Many have lost this experience by listening to the perverted teachings of false shepherds and remaining in sectism. God says the "anointing" breaks and destroys the yoke, and no sect yoke will ever again fit on the neck of a sanctified person, if such remains loyal to the Holy Spirit. Praise God! He alone can effect perfect unity in us, by his divine process--sanctification. Then by the careful adherence to the teachings of God's word this beautiful apostolic unity can be maintained and demonstrated among men, and the prayer of Jesus further answered, "That the world may believe that thou hast sent me."

=The difference between present and future perfection.= In his letter to the church at Philippi, the apostle speaks of a perfection in the future, which unless understood may confuse some minds upon this subject. In Phil. 3:12 he writes, "Not as though I had already attained, either were already perfect: but I follow after, if that I may apprehend that for which also I am apprehended of Christ Jesus." Here it sounds as though perfection is not attainable in this life, but if we notice the language of the context we can clearly see that he is speaking of the resurrection of the dead. Ver. 11. It is the resurrection perfection that he here has reference to, which cannot be attained in this life. We must wait with the apostle until this "mortality shall be swallowed up of life," before we reach a state of absolute perfection, and with him, "press toward the mark for the prize of the high calling of God in Christ Jesus." But in verse 15 he says, "Let us therefore as many as be perfect be thus minded," showing that there is a present perfection which he, with others, has already attained. This is the experience which it is the will of God for us all to enjoy. For by one offering he hath perfected forever them that are sanctified. Dear reader, have you attained it, or are you yet living beneath your blood-bought privilege? "Now the God of peace, that brought again from the dead our Lord Jesus, that great shepherd of the sheep, through the blood of the everlasting covenant, make you perfect in every good work to do his will, working in you that which is well-pleasing in his sight, through Jesus Christ; to whom be glory forever and ever. Amen."--Heb. 13:20, 21.

CHAPTER IX

Holiness

=Holiness an attribute of God.= "Who is like unto thee, O Lord, among the gods? who is like thee, glorious in holiness, fearful in praises, doing wonders?"--Ex. 15:11. "And one cried unto another, and said, Holy, holy, holy, is the Lord of hosts: the whole earth is full of his glory."--Isa. 6:3. "And the four beasts had each of them six wings about him; and they were full of eyes within: and they rest not day and night, saying, Holy, holy, holy, Lord God Almighty, which was, and is, and is to come."--Rev. 4:8.

=God must be worshiped in holiness.= "Give unto the Lord the glory due unto his name: bring an offering and come before him: worship the Lord in the beauty of holiness."--1 Chron. 16:29. "Sing unto the Lord, O ye saints of his, and give thanks at the remembrance of his holiness."--Psa. 30:4.

=God's throne and dwelling-place.= "God reigneth over the heathen: God sitteth upon the throne of his holiness."--Psa. 47:8. "For thus saith the high and lofty One that inhabiteth eternity, whose name is Holy; I dwell in the high and holy place, with him also that is of a contrite and humble spirit."--Isa. 57:15. "Be silent, O all flesh, before the Lord: for he is raised up out of his holy habitation."--Zech. 2:13. "Look down from heaven, and behold from the habitation of thy holiness and thy glory."--Isa. 63:15.

=Holiness becomes God's house.= "Thy testimonies are very sure: holiness becometh thine house, O Lord, forever."--Psa. 93:5. "The aged women likewise, that they be in behavior as becometh holiness."--Titus 2:3.

=The church of God is called a mountain of holiness.= "The Lord bless thee, O habitation of justice, and mountain of holiness."--Jer. 31:23. "Thus saith the Lord; I am returned unto Zion, and will dwell in the midst of Jerusalem: and Jerusalem shall be called a city of truth; and the mountain of the Lord of hosts the holy mountain."--Zech. 8:3. "The wolf and the lamb shall feed together, and the lion shall eat straw like the bullock: and the dust shall be the serpent's meat. They shall not hurt nor destroy in all my holy mountain saith the Lord."--Isa. 65:25.

=God speaks in holiness.= "God hath spoken in his holiness; I will rejoice."--Psa. 60:6. "Mine heart within me is broken because of the prophets; all my bones shake; I am like a drunken man, and like a man whom wine hath overcome, because of the Lord, and because of the words of his holiness."--Jer. 23:9.

=The way of holiness.= "And an highway shall be there, and a way, and it shall be called The way of holiness; the unclean shall not pass over it; but it shall be for those; the wayfaring men, though fools, shall not err therein. No lion shall be there, nor any ravenous beast shall go up thereon, it shall not be found there; but the redeemed shall walk there and the ransomed of the Lord shall return, and come to Zion with songs and everlasting joy upon their heads: they shall obtain joy and gladness, and sorrow and sighing shall flee away."--Isa. 35:8-10.

=The courts of holiness.= "But they that have gathered it shall eat it, and praise the Lord; and they that have brought it together shall drink it in the courts of my holiness."--Isa. 62:9.

=The people of God are holy.= "The people of thy holiness have possessed but a little while: our adversaries have trodden down thy sanctuary."--Isa. 63:18. "And they shall call them, The holy people, The redeemed of the Lord: and thou shalt be called, Sought out, A city not forsaken."--Isa. 62:12. "And the Lord hath avouched thee this day to be his peculiar people, as he hath promised thee, and that thou shouldest keep all his commandments; and to make thee high above all nations which he hath made, in praise, and in name, and in honor; and that thou mayest be an holy people unto the Lord thy God, as he hath spoken."--Deut. 26:18, 19. "But ye are a chosen generation, a royal priesthood, an holy nation, a peculiar people; that ye should show forth the praises of him who hath called you out of darkness into his marvelous light."--1 Pet. 2:9.

=We are called unto holiness.= "Follow peace with all men, and holiness, without which no man shall see the Lord."--Heb. 12:14. "But as he which hath called you is holy, so be ye holy in all manner of conversation; because it is written, Be ye holy, for I am holy."--1 Pet. 1:15, 16. "For God hath not called us unto uncleanness, but unto holiness."--1 Thess. 4:7. "That he would grant unto us, that we being delivered out of the hand of our enemies might serve him without fear, in holiness and righteousness before him, all the days of our life."--Luke 1:74, 75. "For they verily for a few days chastened us after their own pleasure; but he for our profit, that we might be partakers of his holiness."--Heb. 12:10.

=A perfect holiness attainable.= "Having therefore these promises, dearly beloved, let us cleanse ourselves from all filthiness of the flesh and spirit, perfecting holiness in the fear of God."--2 Cor. 7:1.

=Fruit unto holiness.= "But now being made free from sin, and become servants to God, ye have your fruit unto holiness, and the end everlasting life."--Rom. 6:22.

The foregoing scriptures are but a few out of the many plain texts from the word of God teaching us the glorious doctrine of holiness. Some professing Christians look upon this doctrine as unscriptural and impracticable, but in the light of the gospel of Christ there is no other doctrine taught than holiness. The very fact that God, and Jesus Christ, and the Holy Spirit, the word of God, and heaven, and all the celestial hosts are holy, at once suggests to every reasonable mind the utter necessity of holiness in the heart and life of man. The apostle says (Eph. 2:10) that "we are his workmanship, created in Jesus Christ unto good works."

Were we to look upon depraved humanity in the image of Adam, we would see nothing but sin and unholiness; but God has brought into existence a new order of creation in Christ Jesus. The first Adam is a sad and irreparable failure, and in him we see nothing good. All who are living according to the flesh are dead in trespasses and sins, and of course are unholy; but the second Adam, which is Christ has brought redemption and life, in whom there is purity and holiness. The old man is corrupt according to the deceitful lusts, which =must be put off=. The new man is created in righteousness and true holiness, which =must be put on=. The reason some do not comprehend the doctrine of holiness is, they are yet living in the old creation, hence their nature and mind are corrupt. It is utterly impossible for such to be holy in this condition. The command, "Be ye holy," does not apply to them. They are not God's people. The first step for such to take is to repent, which if they obey they will be brought into the kingdom of God's holiness; into the new creation, the workmanship of God in Christ Jesus. Bless the Lord, O my soul, for this new creation of purity and holiness. All the living creatures of heaven bow before him that sitteth upon the throne, saying, Holy, holy, holy! and every sanctified heart on earth can join the blessed anthem of praise and adoration with the consciousness that the all-cleansing blood of Christ has reached its inmost depth and purified it for the habitation of the heavenly guest, the Holy Spirit. The pure heart is God's dwelling-place on earth. Jesus says (John 14:23) "If a man love me, he will keep my words and my Father will love him, and we will come unto him, and make our abode with him."

* * * * *

Thus we see that God not only dwells in the high and holy heaven, but also upon earth in the hearts of his obedient people. Who could consistently believe that God would dwell in a corrupt heart? "He shall be in you," is the promise of Jesus. "At that day [the day when the Holy Spirit comes into the heart], ye shall know that I am in my Father, and ye in me, and I in you." Oh, the depths of the riches of this wonderful redemption, that God would forgive the guilty sinner, then purify his heart and make it his earthly abode. This is his will toward every son and daughter of Adam's race. He will create us in the image of Christ, so that we may truly serve him without fear, in holiness and righteousness before him all the days of our life. This can be called none other than the way of holiness. It is God's own way, and is truly a highway too high for anything unclean to pass over. It is on a perfect level with heaven itself, and yet it is a highway here upon earth for all the ransomed of the Lord to travel upon. It is so plain and simple that no one need be led astray. The wayfaring men though fools, shall not err therein. A wayfaring man means one who is on the way, one who lives on the way. A seafaring man is one who lives on the sea. This way is so safe that though a man may be simple in the estimation of the world, and may be called a fool, yet if he keeps obedient to God he shall not be led astray. "No lion shall be there, nor any ravenous beast shall go up thereon." This indicates a very safe way, where we need not fear any evil. Everything of the flesh or the old man is ruled out, and none but the redeemed shall walk there. We see therefore from the description of the prophet that this is a highway, a clean way, a simple way, a safe way, a way of songs and everlasting joy, which necessarily constitutes a way of holiness.

This is the way upon which the people of God are truly returning to Zion. This Zion is the scriptural name of the church of God. The people of God have been led into captivity of ecclesiastical bondage (Babylon), and the pure light of the gospel of holiness has been darkened by the creeds and doctrines of men, but God is revealing to his own that sanctification is a Bible doctrine; they seek for, and obtain it, and thereby every sectarian yoke is broken, his people find themselves upon this highway of holiness and at home in Zion, the church, free from the bondage of sectism. This is the work of God himself, and will not cease until every one of his people are brought home to Zion, upon the way of holiness. This is the highway that is left for the remnant of his people. Isa. 11:16. This remnant shall be gathered out of all the creeds of men into the one fold, into the true unity of Christ. "For both he that sanctifieth and they who are sanctified are all of one."

The prophet foresaw this blessed return of the people of God and tells us "they shall call them, The holy people." There are some who call themselves holiness people, but the prophet says we shall be called, "The holy people." Holiness factions and sects have actually sprung into existence, which declare that sectism and division is necessary. This class of holiness is not that described in the foregoing scriptures. Bible holiness will in every individual instance destroy everything out of men's hearts that separates or divides. Divisions are the outgrowth of carnality and not of the Spirit of God. Every profession of holiness, therefore, which sanctions division and sectism cannot possibly be the holiness of the Bible. This may seem to some a strong assertion, but it will stand the test of the word of God.

No scriptural unity will ever be effected among the people of God outside the experience of sanctification. Men have repeatedly laid other foundations, but all to no avail. It is a source of great satisfaction to know that wherever the Holy Spirit has the right of way in the hearts of men, there is found true apostolic unity, both in spirit and in doctrine. This is a well authenticated fact which is demonstrated in thousands of hearts today. The holy people are one people, and all are willing to be measured by all of the word of God, which proves to the "profitable for doctrine, for reproof, for correction, for instruction in righteousness. That the man of God may be perfect, thoroughly furnished unto all good works." The apostle teaches us, in Heb. 12:10, that God imparts unto us his holiness: we are partakers of it. It is not an experience which we by our efforts can attain to, but upon the clearly defined conditions of his word we come into possession of his holiness. It is all wrought within us by himself.

"Not by works of righteousness which we have done, but according to his mercy he saved us, by the washing of regeneration, and renewing of the Holy Ghost." Bible holiness is truly an imported article directly from God out of heaven. Some imported goods in this country are much more expensive and of better quality than those of home manufacture. Many of our people prefer to pay the extra expense in order to obtain the better quality, and usually are abundantly satisfied with their purchase. This may serve to illustrate this blessed holiness of the Bible. Men's professions are sometimes like an inferior homemade piece of goods. It soon wears threadbare and betrays its quality, but the genuine imported article of Bible holiness proves satisfactory in every respect, and the more it is worn the better it becomes. It has cost us everything, but it proves to be worth more than everything to us. The reason why some people have failed to get it is, they are unwilling to pay the price. They are deceived by the false doctrine that they do not need to consecrate their all, and hence have accepted a holiness manufactured by man, a homemade article which will never stand the test. A definite, absolute consecration to the loss of all things will never fail to procure the genuine article of true Bible holiness, which will stand the wear of every trial of life and the test of the judgment.

CHAPTER X

The Vine and the Branches

"I am the true vine, and my Father is the husbandman. Every branch in me that beareth not fruit he taketh away; and every branch that beareth fruit, he purgeth it, that it may bring forth more fruit. Now ye are clean through the word which I have spoken unto you. Abide in me, and I in you. As the branch cannot bear fruit of itself, except it abide in the vine; no more can ye, except ye abide in me. I am the vine, ye are the branches: he that abideth in me, and I in him, the same bringeth forth much fruit: for without me ye can do nothing. If a man abide not in me, he is cast forth as a branch, and is withered; and men gather them, and cast them into the fire, and they are burned. If ye abide in me, and my words abide in you, ye shall ask what ye will, and it shall be done unto you. Herein is my Father glorified, that ye bear much fruit; so shall ye be my disciples."--John 15:1-8.

* * * * *

This beautiful analogy teaches us an important lesson. The standard of sanctification is clearly exemplified in the relation between the vine and the branches. Christ is the vine, and every individual Christian is an individual branch; every branch is an individual member of the vine, and every Christian is an individual member of Christ.

* * * * *

What a clear view of the church, and how plainly we can see that there is but one. Every regenerate soul is by one Spirit baptized into this one body. This vine is cared for and kept by God himself, who is the husbandman. Every branch must be a living, fruit-bearing one. It is placed into the vine by the hand which will care for it, and give it every necessary treatment to cause it to bring forth much fruit. If it bears fruit it will be kept in the vine; if it does not bear fruit it will be taken away. The same life which flows through the vine also flows into the branches. It is the branches that bear the fruit. It is the part of the vine to sustain the branches, and the part of the branches to bear fruit. The fruit is the production of the vine-life in the branches. The word of God teaches us that Christ is pure and holy, and in Rom. 11:16 we are taught that if the root be holy, so are the branches. The manner of the induction of the branches into the vine is illustrated by the process of grafting. We are not grown into Christ, but grafted into him. The natural branches of a vine grow out of the vine, and accordingly bear the vine-fruit, but by grace we are grafted into Christ, the vine, and bear the vine-fruit.

A certain writer who advocates the repression theory of sanctification says: "But if I want a tree wholly made good I take it when young and, cutting the stem off on the ground, I graft just where it emerges from the soil; I watch over every bud which the old nature could possibly put forth until the flow of sap from the old roots into the new stem is so complete that the old life has, as it were, been entirely conquered and covered of the new. Now I have a tree entirely renewed--emblem of a Christian who has learned in entire consecration to surrender everything for Christ, and in a whole-hearted faith wholly to abide in him. If in this case the old tree were a reasonable being that could co-operate with the gardener, what would the gardener's language be to it? Would it not be this: 'Yield now thyself entirely to this new nature with which I have invested thee; repress every tendency of the old nature to give buds or sprouts; let all thy sap and all thy life-powers rise up into this graft from yonder beautiful tree which I have put on thee, so shalt thou bring forth sweet and much fruit.' And the language of the tree to the gardener would be: 'When thou graftest me, oh, spare not a single branch, let everything of the old self, even the smallest bud, be destroyed, that I may no longer live in my own, but in that other life that was cut off and brought and put upon me that I might be wholly new and good.' And once again, could you afterwards ask the renewed tree, as it was bearing abundant fruit, what it could say of itself, its answer would be this: 'In me (that is, my roots) there dwelleth no good thing; I am ever inclined to evil; the sap I collect from the soil is in its nature corrupt, and ready to show itself in bearing evil fruit. But just where the sap rises into the sunshine to ripen into fruit, the wise gardener hath clothed me with a new life through which my sap is purified and all my powers are renewed to the bringing forth of good fruit.'"

This author has entirely reversed the scriptural order of grafting in his application of the graft and root, and has illustrated the relation of Christ and the believer by the natural grafting process which can in no sense scripturally apply to this holy relation. Christ is the vine or root, and not the graft. The natural process of grafting is to graft the good graft into a poor root. The graft will grow into a tree and bear the same kind of fruit as the tree from which it was taken, and thus the gardener increases the production of good fruit. But the divine process of grafting is just the reverse. In Rom. 11:24 the apostle says we are grafted into the olive tree (Christ) "contrary to nature." The husbandman takes the penitent sinner out of the kingdom of darkness and translates him into the kingdom of his dear Son. In this regeneration process the sinner (the graft) that was sinful and bore fruit is by God's own process grafted into Christ, the holy vine, and from thence to bear holy fruit. This is certainly a great mystery, like all the works of God's grace, and is indeed contrary to nature, but in perfect conformity with the plan of redemption.

Now, in this condition, there is a certain requirement of the graft necessary that it may bear the vine-fruit; it must =abide= in the vine. This abiding requires a careful watchfulness lest there might be some sprout of the old inward nature, which yet exists within the newly grafted branch, which would spring up and hinder the perfect fruit-bearing of the vine-life. And in this early life, in this new relation of the branch with the vine, it is an attested fact that in quantity this fruit production is more or less hindered by the presence of the old inward nature, in the branch, which if permitted to sprout and grow would certainly prevent the growth of the vine-fruit entirely, and thereby cause the branch to be cut off. That the branch is in the vine there can be no question, for its environments are completely changed and it finds itself a stranger to all of its former associations, customs, and habits. That the vine-life is in the branch there can equally be no question, for the branch has the inward consciousness bearing witness that it belongs to the vine, and it enjoys the sweet fellowship of the vine and all its branches. Also it bears the vine-fruit which brings upon itself the approval of the husbandman.

But this early and new relationship is only the justified life of the branch. The standard of sanctification of the author from whom we have just quoted is in no respect any higher than this, and were it not that there is a higher standard taught in this lesson and in many other scriptures, we would have to be satisfied with justification only.

"Every branch that beareth fruit, he purgeth it, that it may bring forth more fruit." This purging is another process quite contrary to nature, for the term signifies an inward cleansing. A vine-dresser can prune or trim a branch and thereby practically make it clean outwardly from all unnecessary or harmful sprouts which would hinder it from bearing fruit, but there is no known natural process by which the grafted branch could have its inward conditions changed which would affect its nature.

We can see clearly that the entire process of grafting the inferior branch into the good root, and the subsequent purging is wholly contrary to nature, for no man with an object of profit would do any such grafting, neither could anyone reasonably expect the inward conditions of such a graft to become changed.

This purging is wrought within for the purpose of an increase of holy fruit. How beautifully it pictures the experience of sanctification, and subsequent work wrought in the soul of the justified fruit-bearing child of God. It is not a pruning of any unholy sprouts, for they are to be wholly kept from sprouting in the process of the life of bearing holy fruit in this justified relation. The branch is now bearing the very fruit of the holy root, but there is something to be done in it that it may bring forth more fruit; it must be purged from its inward depraved dispositions which it possessed from its parent stock--its "old man ... that the body of sin might be destroyed." Before the purging there was much time and energy occupied in keeping its depraved nature from sprouting. The holy nature of the root was indeed being manifested in the production of holy fruit which was a source of satisfaction, but there was that inward consciousness of an unfavorable condition which hindered the root-life from producing in the branch the quantity necessary to the perfect satisfaction of the husbandman, the vine or the branch.

But now what a glorious change: the old nature is entirely gone, and the sweet soul-rest which the purged branch now enjoys is beyond the power of mortal to express; it can now repose itself so sweetly in the holy vine in its perfectly consecrated life, without any inward hindrance to a perfect flow of the vine-life through its entire being. It can now bring forth more fruit, for every energy from the root is sent direct into the fruit-buds of the branch, and the result is glorious. This purging is just what perfects the inward harmony of the branch with the vine. It could not continue very long in the abiding condition without a consciousness of the need of the purging process. This process becomes a necessity to every branch which abides. "He that abideth in me, and I in him, the same bringeth forth much fruit," which is equivalent to the text, "Every branch that beareth fruit, he purgeth it, that it may bring forth more fruit." It is purged that it may bring forth "more fruit," and now the object of purging is realized, it brings forth "much fruit." Thank God for the purging, the subsequent work in the heart!

The apostles had not yet received this experience. They were clean through the word which Jesus had spoken unto them, to the extent of their knowledge and experience. Unquestionably they were clean from guilt and condemnation, for they were taken out from the world--were no more of it, and the world hated them. They were living in perfect obedience to all the known word of God and were clean through that word, but they had not had the pentecostal purging, "purifying their hearts by faith," as Peter himself testifies of the sanctification of himself and all who were at Pentecost, as well as the experience of Cornelius and his household.

Truly we have much reason to praise God for his wonderful grace in which he brings man, his fallen creature, into such a position that he may become a son of God, then made pure from all the depraved dispositions of his fallen nature. "If a man therefore purge himself from these, he shall be a vessel unto honor, sanctified, and meet for the Master's use, and prepared unto every good work."--2 Timothy 2:21.

CHAPTER XI

Some Helpful Thoughts on Consecration

The experience of sanctification is obtained upon the conditions of definite consecration and faith. In every consecration the soul reaches a point where it must either go through to the death, or else go back and lose the grace of God entirely. The Holy Spirit will make it plain what this death implies, and at last the dying soul goes through its last struggle and yields up its last treasure. When this point is reached and passed, the Holy Spirit will bear witness that the demands of God are now fully met. When Moses had completed the work of building the tabernacle and had placed everything in its proper order, as God commanded him, it is said that "Moses finished the work." So it can be said of us and so each of us can personally testify by the witness of the Spirit bearing witness with our spirit in this absolute and definite consecration, that we have "finished the work." Every doubt as to the completion of this consecration is banished, and has no room to exist in our hearts, for we know that it is complete. We can so sweetly and willingly say, "Thy will be done," with a most delightful consciousness that all the past, present, and future, of all that pertains to our life, is yielded up to his blessed will. Nothing on earth is held half so sweet and precious as his will.

We can realize down deep in our souls what Jesus meant when he gave himself to sanctify us and said, "I come to do thy will." We can enter into the fellowship of his sufferings and death, for all that we have and are, and all that we expect to be in the future, and all that we know and ever expect to know, are now forever and eternally yielded up to that precious will of God. It required the will of Jesus to be yielded up to death to do the will of the Father that we might be sanctified, and it equally requires our will to be yielded up to death and the loss of all things, that we might be sanctified. It required his will even to the death to obtain it for us, and it requires our will even to death to receive it from him. Yes, dear reader, a real death; so real that it includes everything, and it can only be said of us as it was said of the Colossian saints, "Ye are dead, and your life is hid with Christ in God."

This death consecration is beautifully typified in the consecration and sanctification of the priests of the Old Testament dispensation. In Lev. 8 we read that Moses was commanded of the Lord to take Aaron and his sons and three animals with him. The blood of one of these animals was to be shed for the sin-offering; one for the "burnt offering," and one for the "consecration" offering. The blood of each was shed and applied separately for a special purpose. Each finds its antitype in the precious blood of Jesus, who offered himself without spot to God that he might sanctify the church. The blood of the sin-offering provides for that part of our nature which would naturally reach out and cling to those things which are sinful. In every justified heart which is not yet wholly sanctified there exists such a principle which in itself is depraved and sinful, and were it permitted to respond to the sinful things without, it would bring the believers into transgression. This is the "body of sin," or "our old man," which according to the law of the Spirit of life in Christ Jesus, must be destroyed and cleansed out. This existing in the heart, if unrestrained, is the fruitful soil out of which grows every evil work. We can see its productions in many different aspects in the religious world today. Every sect on earth is a production of this body of sin. Every manifestation of carnal division is some of its evil fruits. Everything that is in the least degree contrary to the pure word of God, whether it be word or deed, is but the outgrowth of this evil thing, which was created and planted into the hearts of Adam and Eve by the devil, and has become the dominating characteristic of depraved humanity. Justification does not cleanse this out of the heart. It only takes away the guilt and trespasses of the sinner, and brings him into the favor of God, who gave his Son a "trespass-offering" for the world. But Jesus gave himself a "sin-offering" for the church, and when the heart has yielded up to the death for the destruction of this depravity it can truly be said of such an one that we are dead to sin, for the blood of Jesus in this sin-offering will most certainly effect this cleansing.

But a true Bible consecration includes something more than a yielding up of the heart for the cleansing out of this sin principle. In the type, we see there was another animal sacrificed in this consecration service. It was the one for the "burnt offering." The blood of this sacrifice corresponds with the sacrifice of the blood of Jesus which also provides for the cleansing of that part of our nature that clings to the things of life which in themselves are not sinful but are God-given blessings. Our unsanctified affections must also become purified from every taint of depravity. That this may be accomplished, it becomes necessary that the heart yield up to the death every cherished object, even though it be a God-given blessing; it must be yielded up and laid upon the altar as a "burnt offering." The affections cannot be purified until the object of the affections is yielded. We cannot perfectly obey the first and great commandment, "Thou shalt love the Lord thy God with all thy heart, and with all thy soul, and with all thy mind, and with all thy strength," until every affection is fully taken off from every object of earth and placed upon God exclusively. This means that we willingly lay upon the altar our loved ones, no matter how sacred or precious they may be--father, mother, brother, sister, husband, wife, children, home, property, reputation, and everything within the scope of our earthly existence. All henceforth and forever yielded up to God, no more to be ours, as really and as perfectly as though we were breathing our last upon our death-bed, and then in due time we were laid into our coffin, the lid fastened down, and lowered into the grave, the grave filled up and nothing left but a mound to mark where our earthly remains lie. Or, to view the subject from another standpoint, this yielding up must be as real as though our loved ones and every cherished treasure of earth were laid upon the altar, to be offered up a burnt sacrifice. In due time the fire will be kindled, and our cherished objects will one by one be consumed into smoke and finally all will disappear, a consumed sacrifice unto the Lord.

A quarter of a century ago my own precious mother was brought to this consecration. She was shown by the Holy Spirit that she did not have her children perfectly yielded up to the Lord. She was praying for their conversion. At last she became willing to lay them upon the altar and she did it thoroughly. She gave them to the Lord a living sacrifice. In a short time her four oldest were converted, and in due time the two others as they grew up were also brought into the fold of Christ. She rejoiced and praised God for this and often expressed herself that her children were not her own, they were the Lord's, for his service or sacrifice, just as he should see proper. At last this consecration was brought to the test. The Lord began to kindle the fire to consume the "burnt offering." He laid his hand upon one and took her home to heaven. Then another, and sent him thousands of miles away to preach the gospel in regions beyond. Then another, and sent him far distant in another direction to labor in the gospel vineyard. Then another, and sent her still another direction to publish the word of God; and as these cherished objects thus vanished out of her sight she could say, "They are the Lord's, not mine." In one of her letters she wrote me these words: "Well, my dear boy, I truly realized what it meant years ago to lay my dear children upon the altar of the Lord: but now I realize what it means to see them consumed into smoke."

Dear brother and sister, this is what a burnt offering means, and how good our heavenly Father is to require this sacrifice of us! Oh, how many sad heartaches it saves us! How many bitter tears of anguish and sorrow! I have stood at the open grave where a poor grief-stricken mother wrung her hands and cried out, "Oh, I cannot, I cannot give up my precious darling. Let me be buried with it--I cannot be parted from it!" I have also stood at another grave, where the form of a consecrated loved one was sinking out of human sight. The mother stood gazing at the object of earth as it was laid back to dust, then with her eyes turned toward heaven she said, "Dear Lord, thou hast only taken thine own to thyself; my heart feels the parting pangs, but I say willingly, 'Thy will be done.'"

Ah, what a contrast! The one mother knew nothing of this blessed consecration, the other did. The one had but little grace to sustain her in her bereavement, the other had the abounding grace, for she had already yielded up her sacred treasures to the Lord. The one buried all her comfort and hope in the grave, the other simply buried a lifeless form of clay; though sacred and precious to her heart, yet she had consecrated it to the Lord, and now in seeing it vanish out of her sight, she could feel that it was not her own. The one returned to her empty home with her heart full of sorrow, the other returned in the comfort of Him who comforteth us in all our tribulations. She had paid the price of =her all=, and now she enjoys the blessing of =Jesus' all=--the abiding of his glorious presence, which comforts her heart and home, and fills the emptiness with himself and his bountiful grace.

Oh, how beautiful and reasonable to consecrate everything that our affections have held sacred and dear, to him. We all know very well that all these treasures of earth are of no enduring substance. No matter how much they may be to us, they in due time will either vanish out of our sight, or else we will have to leave them. How much better, and how much more satisfactory it is to yield them all up to Jesus, to whom they rightly belong, and who has only loaned them to us in the first place. He is justly entitled to all of our affections, for what has he not yielded up that was due to himself, that he might purchase this glorious grace for us? Now he wants the supremacy in our hearts' affections, so that he can fashion us according to himself through and through, and impart his own nature into our affections, that we may henceforth love with his love, those sacred treasures around which our affections have so entwined, and claimed as ours. Before our consecration we loved him, but these other objects of our love were between us and him. They hindered our love towards him, and equally hindered his love from perfectly flowing into our hearts. We loved him, and realized that he loved us, but it was not perfect; there were objects in our way, and there were objects in his way. These objects were our sacred treasures. Depravity had affected our affections so that we could not hold these treasures as we should. But now what a satisfactory change! We yielded all these objects to him, and took him in their stead. Now he occupies the place. He owns our treasures, and we own him. But what of our treasures? We have them all back again, through him. Before our consecration, they were between us and him. Now he is between us and them, and with him he freely gives us all things. He can use all of these things according to his own good pleasure, making any disposition of them which might seem good in his sight, for they are his, not ours. If he should place us over them as his stewards, then we hold them in trust for him and do with them just as he orders, and when, one by one, they consume away on the altar of his service, or, if according to his sovereign will, he shall remove them out of our sight, we can say, "Amen, Lord, thy will be done."

Now, in the act of Bible consecration, the believer may not realize all of this, and the utmost depth of the cleansing that has been wrought in the heart and affections, or the difference between the sin-offering and the burnt offering, but it will not be long afterward, until the knowledge of this cleansing shall begin to dawn upon us and our soul becomes more and more enraptured in this glorious experience of sanctification. But we see in the type still another animal to be slain--the consecration offering. The blood of this animal was applied to the body of Aaron and his sons. First it was put upon the tips of their right ears, the thumbs of their right hands, and the great toes of their right feet. Then afterwards it was sprinkled with the anointing oil upon Aaron and his garments too, and upon his sons and their garments. This ceremonial process was the completion of their sanctification. The blood of this consecration offering corresponds with the blood of Jesus which provides for the sanctification of our body. In this consecration we not only offer up our hearts and affections to Jesus, but we also present our bodies a living sacrifice. This includes our all, spirit, soul and body. Our ears, hands, and feet, our entire physical being, is dedicated henceforth to his service, to labor and suffer hardships, to be used in sacrifice, or service, either at the martyrs' stake or on the gospel altar, any way, and every way, in which he may order it for his own honor and glory. These eyes shall see, this tongue shall speak, this mind shall think, these ears shall hear, these hands shall labor, these feet shall run, this strength and these energies, this heart shall beat, every faculty, organ, and appetite shall be used only for him, who has so freely given himself for us; and thus this body becomes the temple, and the earthly dwelling-place of the Holy Ghost, his own exclusive dedicated property. While it is not possible that we could itemize these things in the consecration of our bodies, there is a yielding up of our all which sweeps the scope and brings the witness of the Spirit that our consecration is complete and we have "finished the work." We are now upon believing grounds, and faith can appropriate the power of the all-cleansing blood.

"By faith I venture on his word, My doubts are o'er, the vict'ry won, He said the altar sanctifies, I just believe him and 'tis done."

CHAPTER XII

Questions and Answers

Question. How may we know definitely that we are sanctified?

Answer. We may know it by knowing that we have met all the conditions. This grace is obtained upon the conditions of consecration and faith. When we are sure that we have measured up to a true Bible consecration, we will have no difficulty in knowing that we are sanctified. The depth of meaning of this consecration does not necessarily need to be fully comprehended by the seeker, as we enter into this covenant, but there is a yielding up of ourself and entire all, to the known and unknown will of God, to an extent that covers everything.

God knows when we have reached and passed this point, and it will not be long before the Holy Spirit will definitely witness to us that the consecration is complete, and the covenant ratified by this glorious indwelling consciousness.

This consecration may be illustrated by the contract and union of holy matrimony. When the bride and groom enter into the covenant according to God's word, they have little knowledge of the obligations they are taking upon themselves. They know nothing of the detailed realities of life; its joys and sorrows, hardships and trials that are before them; but they know that they dearly love each other, and have not the slightest fear in yielding themselves to each other completely and exclusively, so long as they both shall live. They enter into this covenant with all good confidence that the object of their love will not require anything hard or impossible, and as the future realities of life unfold and one by one they meet the many responsibilities that the covenant implies, they find that their love is equal to the responsibility, and as long as they continue to love each other they will never have the slightest disposition to break that marriage covenant.

So the heart which makes the consecration for sanctification will not comprehend the great scope of its meaning at the time of entering into this covenant, but if we love Jesus as we should we will not fear what he may require of us in the details of his will in the future. We are already enraptured with his love. He has proved himself to be a loving and faithful Redeemer in dying for us, and now as we see he requires us to yield ourselves even to death for him, we can confidently enter into the conditions of this covenant with the assurance that he will demand nothing of us beyond the power of the love to fulfill.

Yes, we will know definitely when our consecration is complete, and then we will have no trouble to believe in the promises for the cleansing. As Bible repentance is the believing ground for justification, so Bible consecration is the believing ground for sanctification.

Ques. How may we keep sanctified?

Ans. By abiding in the conditions by which we obtained the experience. As long as our consecration remains intact, and our faith remains firm in the promises, we are sanctified, no matter what the assertions of our feelings may be. To cease believing will forfeit our experience. To cease obeying in any respect will produce the same effect; but "if we walk in the light as he is in the light, we have fellowship one with another; and the blood of Jesus Christ his Son cleanseth us from all sin."

Ques. If Jesus was not sanctified until his death, how can we be?

Ans. Jesus was sanctified before his death. He testifies to it in John 10:36. There is a sense in which he was sanctified by his death; that is, he became a perfect redeemer by his death. He set himself apart for this specific purpose. This is the meaning of the saying of Jesus in John 17:19--"And for their sakes I sanctify myself, that they also might be sanctified through the truth." Another scripture, Heb. 5:9 has the same meaning. "And being made perfect, he became the author of eternal salvation unto all them that obey him." In the use of the terms "sanctify" and "perfect" we could by no means infer that Jesus was not pure and holy before his suffering on the cross. He became a perfect Saviour by his death and through suffering. It is absurd and casts a reflection upon the redemption plan, to say that Jesus was not holy until resurrection. In this sense only was he made "perfect" by his death. As to his people being holy and sanctified in this life, we have the whole word of God in favor of such a life. Thank God, it is his will that we should live "in holiness and righteousness before him all the days of our life." It does require a death on our part to obtain this glorious grace. In this respect we must die to get it. Jesus died to purchase it for us. We must die to receive it--not a literal death, but a death to sin and the world. The river of Jordan truly signifies a death, but we can cross over it and remain in this mortal life. The land of Canaan is the land of holiness, which all of God's people can enter into and possess in this life.

Ques. Does not the Bible say, "If we say that we have no sin we deceive ourselves and the truth is not in us"?

Ans. Yes, but this does not teach us that we cannot be free from sin. If we were to take this verse by itself without its context we might have a scripture contradictory to the word of God, but if we read the seventh and ninth verses with the eighth verse of 1 John 1, we see plainly by these three verses connected that we can be cleansed from all sin and unrighteousness. This verse implies that if any one who has not been cleansed from sin should say he has no sin to be cleansed from, he deceives himself.

Ques. Do we not grow into sanctification and therefore reach it gradually?

Ans. No; this would be contrary to the plan of redemption. We do not grow =into= any of the graces. We are commanded to grow IN grace. The grace of pardon and justification is imparted by the Holy Spirit. We can grow in this grace and in the knowledge of our Lord and Saviour which, if we do, will soon bring us to the knowledge of our need of purity and sanctification, and we will see that this is a grace which is intended for us. We gladly comply with the conditions for the same, and enter into it by faith. God now performs the work in our hearts by the power of his Holy Spirit. We cannot do it ourselves, only in the sense that we meet the required conditions. It is impossible for us to grow into purity. This is beyond our individual power; it requires the power of God. We purify ourselves by making the separation of everything outwardly; God then purifies our hearts by an instantaneous work of grace. This grace by no means implies a maturity in growth. It only brings us into a position where we can the more rapidly grow up in spiritual things.

Ques. Why do we not get it all when we are justified?

Ans. Because the conditions for the two graces are not the same. The penitent sinner cannot, in his sinful condition, meet the requirements for sanctification, and God does not mean that he should. All that the sinner can possibly do is to repent. When he has fully repented, then he can believe on the Lord Jesus Christ and receive his pardon. This is justification. He is justified from all his sins through true repentance and faith. Those are the Scriptural conditions for justification, but the conditions for sanctification are consecration and faith. Repentance and consecration are vastly different. The first means to give up all sinful things, with a godly sorrow for all sins committed, and a solemn determination that by the grace of God all sinning shall forever cease. The second means to yield up to God all our good things, every sacred treasure of our heart and affections, with our body and every ransomed power, as a living sacrifice. The first is God's requirement of every sinner. The second is his requirement of every justified believer. The first is all that the guilty sinner can possibly comprehend. The second is that which only the justified believer can comprehend. Therefore it is utterly impossible for us to get sanctified at the time of our justification. The two are distinct and separate works of grace, obtained upon distinct and separate conditions.

Some people have vainly believed, and some vainly teach, that there is but one work of grace; but such a doctrine is contrary to the word of God, the conditions of the plan of redemption, and the glorious testimonies of thousands of saints who have lived in the past and those who are living witnesses today. It is perfectly natural and logical to every honest and willing child of God who is not yet sanctified to soon believe that there is a second work of grace. Perhaps it will take a few months for some to find out their need, but it is only a question of time till every one will find an inward longing for something more, to satisfy the inward condition of the heart. To prove this statement let us listen to the testimonies of those who are simply justified and have had no teaching on sanctification, whether their Christian life be one of years or but a few months. Everyone who stands in this justified relation with God gives expression in some respects according to the following: "I thank God for salvation and am not sorry that I ever gave my heart to God, but I do feel the need of a deeper work of grace." Another will say, "Pray for me that I may have a clean heart." Another will request prayer for perfect love; another will confess to having been overcome by sin, and having made some crooked paths, and feels sorry and wants to get nearer to God and get a better experience.

Now we cannot doubt the sincerity of these hearts, neither their experience. Their experiences are those of honest, willing children of God who are anxious to do the whole will of God. Such expressions would not be given by professors who are void of salvation. The fact is, the experiences of these hearts teach them the need of the second grace, and unless they should be deceived by some false doctrines, they would keep on with such testimonies until they should obtain that perfect love, or a clean heart, or a deeper work of grace.

Do they not testify that the first work of grace is not deep enough? They are glad for the first work, but they want something deeper. They are glad that grace has found their heart, but they want a clean heart--one that is free from those conscious uprisings of evil which, if unrestrained, would bring them into condemnation and guilt, and perhaps have already overcome them and produced such an effect in their lives. They are glad for the sweet love of God that has found its way into their hearts, but they long for perfect love. They are conscious of some obstacles which hinder that love from being perfect, and yet they do not understand just how those obstacles can be removed. Someone may tell them that they have all they can get from God and to ask for more would be presumption, and yet their souls cry out for that which is natural in the grace of God, and how ready they are, when they hear sanctification taught, to meet the conditions and enter into the rest for their souls--this perfect love, this deeper work of grace, and this experience of a clean heart, and this baptism with the Holy Ghost.

Now let us listen to their testimonies. What do we hear? Ah, we hear them praising God for this they were so longing for. One will praise God for a clean heart; another will say he has found the perfect love; another will testify to the baptism of the Holy Ghost. Others will thank God for sanctification, and others will call it this sweet soul-rest, etc., which all mean the same blessed experience of sanctification. Now if we ask them if they believe in a second work of grace, what will they answer us? Ah, there is no question about it. They have it in their hearts, and they are spoiled for any argument upon the subject.

So it is with all God's people who have met the definite conditions for sanctification and have come into this precious grace. We know it is a second work.

Ques. How can one keep free from evil thoughts?

Ans. The pure heart and mind do not entertain an evil thought. As soon as such thoughts are presented they are banished. In 2 Cor. 10:5 we read how such things are dealt with. "Casting down imaginations, and every high thing that exalteth itself against the knowledge of God, and bringing into captivity every thought to the obedience of Christ." An evil thought thus captivated does not enter into the heart and therefore does not become a sin to us. The apostle James says, "When lust hath conceived, it bringeth forth sin." The evil thought must first enter into the heart and be conceived into a desire before it becomes sin.

This world is full of sin and iniquity on every hand. We may hear profanity as we pass along the street, or we may see iniquity before our eyes daily as we come in contact with the world, we may pick up a secular paper and read of murder and theft, and thus these evil thoughts may enter into our minds, but they do not conceive or take root in our hearts. They are brought into captivity and banished from us. If when reading or hearing of a murder or theft, someone should see an opportunity to commit a similar deed and resolve in his heart that he would do so at his first opportunity, that person would have conceived the thought in his heart, and in the sight of God he would be a murderer or a thief, even though he never had the opportunity to carry out the design. The heart that is purified by the cleansing blood of Christ and momently kept in the efficacy of that blood, is the sacred dwelling-place of the Holy Spirit, who has the full and exclusive control of the heart.

As long as our will is kept in line with the will of God the Holy Spirit will abide. The word of God says, "Greater is he that is in you than he that is in the world," and, "No man can enter into a strong man's house and spoil his goods, except he will first bind the strong man." The strong man--the Holy Spirit--is in his own house, and it is impossible for sin to enter in unless we by our own will consent to it. The word of God speaks of the Holy Spirit as the seal. This thought is practically illustrated by the common use of a seal in canning fruit. We may be ever so careful with fruit in getting it properly prepared for the can, but if we set it away without the seal, it will not be long until the fruit is spoiled. It requires the seal to keep the fruit from spoiling. There is something in the air which, if not excluded, will spoil the fruit. The use of the seal is to exclude the air.

So it is with our heart. Justification inducts us into Christ; sanctification purifies our hearts and seals us in him; now when sin would come in contact with our hearts and defile it, there is something there, the Holy Spirit, the seal, which keeps sin from entering in. "If we walk in the light, as he is in the light, we have fellowship one with another and the blood of Jesus Christ his Son cleanseth us from all sin."--1 John 1:7. Notice the word "cleanseth." It is in the present tense. By our walking in the light, which signifies our perfect obedience continually to all the known will of God, our heart is kept in line with God's will and hence under the provisions of his grace--the sin-cleansing blood of Jesus. Thus the perpetual cleansing keeps our heart pure. By the inwrought work of sanctification we =obtain= this purity, and by our obedience to God, walking in the light, we =retain= it.

In this blessed grace, no evil thought can enter our heart unless by our consent. We have willed it so that we forsake all sin and turn to God; thus his grace of justification has found its way into our heart. Then by a definite consecration we willed it so that the cleansing blood of Jesus should purify our heart from inborn depravity, and his grace of sanctification has found its way within, and has brought the glorious heavenly guest, the Holy Spirit, there to abide. Now as we continue to walk in this light we are kept from sin. By our will we either open or close our heart toward God. The will is the entrance and door. The grace of God is free, and more abundant than the sunshine that lights and warms this earth. All of this sunshine may be kept out of the room if we will to have it so. We can darken the windows and doors, and keep every ray of light out, or we can have abundant sunshine if we will, by simply removing the obstacles. So it is with the illimitable grace of God. If we open up wide the door of our heart--our will--and keep it open continually, the grace will flow in and keep out everything that is not like heaven. "For God, who commanded the light to shine out of darkness, hath shined in our hearts, to give the light of the knowledge of the glory of God in the face of Jesus Christ. But we have this treasure in earthen vessels, that the excellency of the power may be of God, and not of us."--2 Cor. 4:6, 7.

If we close the door of our heart toward God, it will be opening it toward sin, and the result will be darkness. Depravity will at once have entered in, and then as every evil thought comes into the mind it will find no obstruction to its way into the heart, where it will find a fruitful soil in which to germinate and bring forth evil work.

Ques. Does not the word of God say that "from within, out of the heart of men, proceed evil thoughts," etc.?

Ans. Yes, this is true; but we must consider what kind of heart Jesus is speaking about. Let us turn to Mark 7. The Pharisees and certain scribes found fault because they saw some of Jesus' disciples eat bread without washing their hands; not that their hands were not clean enough to eat with, but because they did not serve the traditional ceremony, thinking that thus the hearts of the disciples were defiled, but Jesus explained that nothing can defile the heart except that which enters into it. Ver. 19. "And he said, That which cometh out of the man, that defileth the man. For from within, out of the heart of men, proceed evil thoughts, adulteries, fornication, murders, thefts, covetousness, wickedness, deceit, lasciviousness, an evil eye, blasphemy, pride, foolishness: all these evil things come from within, and defile the man."--Verses 20-23.

We see that this is a true picture of the unregenerated heart, which has no good thing in it. We also see that it is not an evil thought presented to the mind from without which defileth the man, but it is the evil thought that comes from within a corrupted heart. There are two sources of evil thoughts. 1. The devil himself directly. 2. A corrupt, unregenerate heart, which is a hotbed and nursery of the devil. From either of these outward sources evil thoughts may be presented to the mind of a child of God, but from neither can our hearts be defiled if they are brought into captivity and banished, as will be the case with every obedient soul.

Ques. Is not every mistake a sin?

Ans. No; there are many mistakes which are not sinful. There is no doubt that every sin is a serious mistake, but God's people do not make such mistakes. The word of God teaches what sin is, and if we abide in Christ we will not commit sin. The scriptural definition of sin will help us to understand this. "Therefore to him that knoweth to do good, and doeth it not, to him it is sin."--Jas. 4:17. "All unrighteousness is sin."--1 John 5:17. "When lust hath conceived it bringeth forth sin."--Jas. 1:15. "Sin is the transgression of the law."--1 John 3:4. "Whosoever abideth in him sinneth not."--1 John 3:6. Any mistake that would be a violation of God's law would be a sin, but aside from this, a simple error in judgment is not a sin. Salvation does not warrant an experience beyond the probability of error in our human nature, and Christian perfection is not infallibility.

Ques. Did not Paul say there was sin dwelling in him?

Ans. Yes. This expression we find in Rom. 7:17. The apostle when writing this chapter was not describing his sanctified condition. It is a description of his condition when he was in the flesh, or carnal state. "For when we were in the flesh, the motions of sin, which were by the law, did work in our members to bring forth fruit unto death."--Ver. 5. And in Rom. 8:8, 9 he says, "So then they that are in the flesh cannot please God. But ye are not in the flesh, but in the Spirit, if so be that the Spirit of God dwell in you." "For the law of the Spirit of life in Christ Jesus hath made me free from the law of sin and death."--Ver. 2. Paul's condition when under the law is described in the 7th chapter of Romans. In chapters 6 and 8 he describes the condition of the child of God under grace.

Ques. But does he not say in Rom. 3:10 that "there is none righteous, no, not one"?

Ans. Yes. But he was not describing the condition of the child of God under grace. He refers to the world under the law. No Bible Christian can conscientiously apply Rom. 3:10-18 to himself.

Ques. How about Solomon, who said, "There is not a just man upon the earth, that doeth good, and sinneth not"?

Ans. This also was spoken of the condition of the people under the law. "The law made nothing perfect, but the bringing in of a better hope did by the which we draw nigh unto God."--Heb. 7:19.

In order to properly apply scripture it is very helpful to always consider: 1. Who wrote it? 2. When was it written? 3. Of whom or to whom was it written? In this manner it is easy to determine the meaning of such scriptures as here have been mentioned and many others, which would otherwise render it impossible to harmonize the whole word of God. The two dispensations, the law and grace, are vastly different in many respects. The first was but the shadow of the second. In the first there was no power to take away sin, or to change the inward moral condition of man but in the second there is the power and provision in the redemption of Christ to save us to the uttermost.

Ques. But did not Paul say of himself when under grace that he kept his body under and brought it into subjection? Does not this indicate that his body was yet sinful?

Ans. Let us turn to 1 Cor. 9:25-27. We see here that he makes no reference to his body being sinful, but tells how he practices temperance in all things. Like one who prepares himself for a race, in training himself physically, bringing his body into subjection in everything, that he may be able to win the prize. In sanctification the sinful and depraved nature is destroyed, and everything unholy cleansed out; therefore there are no sinful propensities to be kept down and under, but all sin is kept out. The sanctified body is not sinful but holy (1

Cor. 3:17) and is designed for God for the dwelling-place of his Holy Spirit.

Every propensity and appetite is now restored to its condition of purity, in which it was created before sin entered into the world, but yet we are human. Sanctification does not destroy our human nature, but simply brings it into easy control, with every propensity in harmony with the design of its Creator. But we are yet in this world and the creature--our physical nature--is yet subject to vanity.

Satan with all his malicious and crafty devices is lying in wait to deceive and lead astray. He comes to us and appeals to our physical nature in many respects, and it is necessary that we keep in a watchful and prayerful attitude "lest by any means, as the serpent beguiled Eve through his subtilty, so your minds should be corrupted from the simplicity that is in Christ."--2 Cor. 11:3. Even through our appetites would Satan gain the advantage over us, and finally bring us into bondage, if he were permitted to do so. In this respect the apostle Paul kept his body under and brought every appetite and propensity into subjection to serve him, rather than he should serve them, and all his ransomed powers were bent upon his faithful obedience to the one object of his existence--the ministry of the gospel.

Ques. Can a person lose the experience of sanctification?

Ans. Yes, it is possible to lose it.

This experience does not place us beyond temptation. It only fortifies us more strongly against the world, the flesh, and the devil, and greatly diminishes the probability of falling.

Ques. Does not the word of God teach that "Whosoever abideth in him sinneth not"; and "Whosoever is born of God doth not commit sin"?

Ans. Yes; this is certainly true. There is no possibility of sinning in Christ. It is only when a person gets out of Christ that it is possible to commit sin. The term "born of God" includes both justified and sanctified. No justified person can commit sin and retain the justified experience; therefore, no one who is born of God and retains this divine relationship in him will sin. Everyone who commits sin must do so outside of this life in God. The apostle John says, "Whosoever sinneth hath not seen him, neither known him," which signifies that in the act of committing sin a person gets entirely outside of Christ. In such an act he has not seen, nor known him. The apostle also says concerning those who are born of God, that they "cannot sin," because they are "born of God." This statement agrees with the one just quoted, and proves that it is not possible to commit sin in Christ; but it does not infer that it is not possible to get out of Christ and commit sin. The expression "cannot sin" simply signifies that there is no disposition in the heart to commit sin. We are constrained by love to him who gave his life for us, to do nothing to displease him. We have the privilege and power to displease him if we will, but we have no will to do so. We "cannot" do it and abide loyal to him. A mother may be requested to take a weapon and slay her child, but she at once answers, I cannot! Yea, she can if she will; but the answer would in every case be repeated "I cannot!" It is not difficult to see why she cannot do such a deed. She has no disposition to do so, even though she has the power to do it. Her love for her child renders it impossible so long as that love continues.

Ques. Can a person be restored to this experience of sanctification if it should be lost?

Ans. Yes, by complying with the conditions; but the same act of sin which would cause us to lose our experience of sanctification would also forfeit our justification, and bring us into condemnation. Therefore the conditions necessary to get back into Christ would be first, repentance and faith; then by a definite consecration, or a renewal of our consecration which has been broken, and a definite faith in the all-cleansing blood of Christ we will be restored to sanctification.

Ques. In case a person shall unfortunately sustain such a loss, how long would it take to become restored?

Ans. Just as long as it would take to meet the conditions. No one in such a case should wait an hour, but knowing just what conditions are required, they should be complied with at once.

Ques. How can we understand the seventh chapter of Romans to harmonize with the doctrine of holiness?

Ans. From the seventh verse of this chapter the apostle describes his experience when under the law, before he had been brought into the grace of God. From the seventh to the fourteenth verse he speaks of his experience, making use of the past tense. From the fourteenth verse through the rest of the chapter he makes use of the present tense, but still continues the description of his past experience.

It is held by holiness opposers that this chapter is a description of the apostle's experience under grace, and that this is the highest possible experience attainable in this gospel dispensation. But such an experience is not consistent with grace at all. If this were all that grace can do, there would be no encouragement in it for any one to accept. No sinner could do worse than the experience described here, except that he might deliberately choose to sin and do everything wrong. This chapter describes the sinner as having a desire in his mind to do right but no power within him to carry out his desires, in any respect. He is awakened to the requirements of the law of God, but finds he is held fast by another law which holds him with such power as to render him helpless, utterly helpless, to do anything good. This does not apply to the justified experience under grace. It applies perfectly to that under the law, because the Mosaic law had no other power, nor design, than to awaken the conscience; and this is just what the apostle here describes concerning himself "For I was alive without the law once: but when the commandment came, sin revived, and I died."--Rom. 7:9. He died in trespasses and sin. This was the condition of all men under the law, and this is where grace found the world. "Now we know that what things soever the law saith, it saith to them who are under the law that every mouth may be stopped, and all the world may become guilty before God."--Rom. 3:19.

Ques. Is every child at birth sinful by nature?

Ans. The race of mankind has descended from Adam through Seth, who was born not in the image of God as Adam and Eve were created, but in the image and after the likeness of Adam as he was after the fall. It is evident that our first parents lost the image of God through their disobedience, and it is also evident that this image of God has never been regained through the first Adam. The word of God plainly teaches that Christ, the second Adam, is the image of God, and by the power of his redemption grace, he will restore this image to every son and daughter of Adam's race who will meet the conditions for the same. The first Adam is depraved and a sad failure. He has no power within himself to change his moral condition. The second Adam (Christ) is a glorious success. He possesses all the moral characteristics of purity and holiness that the first Adam did before the fall, and also has the power to impart this image of God to all who come to him.

The image of Adam is entailed upon the race through the fall, and evidently, though mysteriously, affects mankind through the natural law of generation. The image of God is provided for the race through redemption in Christ, and is imparted to each individual through the divine law of regeneration and its accompanying grace. It is compatible with the word of God, with reason, and with observation, that every child born into this world through the natural law of generation, very early in life in a greater or lesser degree manifests some of the characteristics of this image of Adam. Just how, when, and where the child partakes of this nature would be a subject of conjecture and speculation. The psalmist says he was conceived in sin and shapen in iniquity (See Psa. 51:5.) and according to the condition of the unregenerate world this is as true today as it was in the days of David. The innocent child, of course, is not accountable for this inward condition of its nature, but as it grows to the age of accountability it becomes an easy prey to the powers of sin because of this condition. While innocent, it is unquestionably acceptable in the sight of God and comes under the provisions of the redemption of Christ unconditionally:

for "sin is not imputed where there is no law."--Rom. 5:13. The apostle says "I was alive without the law once; but when the commandment came, sin revived, and I died."--Rom. 7:9. He no doubt had reference to the innocent period of his life. The principle of sin was in his nature, but "without the law sin was dead"; it had no power to bring him into condemnation. As soon, however, as he became able to know what the law required of him, sin revived and made him a transgressor by causing him to disobey the commands of God. There is no room to question the fact that sin was in his nature; for he plainly states it so, and the expression, "sin revived" indicates that it had been in him during the period of his innocent state.

CHAPTER XIII

Personal Experience

In conclusion I desire to add my humble testimony of a personal experience of the glorious work of entire sanctification.

At the age of seventeen years I was converted. All who were acquainted with me had no reason to doubt the genuine, inwrought grace of pardon and the new life which at once began to bring forth fruit unto God. But the one to whom this mighty change seemed the most marvelous was myself. My poor soul, which for several years had been held under the terrible bondage and darkness of sin, was now turned from darkness unto light and from the power of Satan unto God, and there was no room either internally or externally to question that I had received forgiveness of sins. The glory and blessedness of that sacred hour and that hallowed spot "when love divine first found me" can never be erased from my memory. I will not say, as I have often heard others testify of their own, that my experience was more wonderful than that of anyone else, but I do not see how it could have been any more wonderful to me than it was, and it is but useless to make an effort to tell it. All who have come into this precious life, and have the Spirit bearing witness with our spirit that we are the children of God, understand what it means to be justified by faith and have this sweet peace with God through our Lord Jesus Christ.

But this peace with God meant war with the enemy of my soul, and I soon learned that the battle was a serious one. The artful schemes of the enemy were deeply planned for my overthrow, and while attending school the spirit of the world succeeded in leading me into defeat, and I decided to yield myself again unto the world, and gave up the struggle against sin. But oh, what darkness! God only knows what horrors I suffered. I had been saved but a few months and had had the taste of true happiness which so spoiled me for the empty pleasures of sin that I was often so wretched and miserable that life was a burden. But thank God, this condition of life was only of about two month's duration. Through the burning tears of my precious mother, which fairly bathed my face and neck one day as she suddenly came into my room and clasped her arms around me, I was enabled again to decide for God and heaven. This decision was so thoroughly burned in upon my soul by those scalding tears that, by the grace of God, I believe it will last from that day to my latest breath. The sweet joy and peace of heaven was restored and I believe I enjoyed salvation as much as anyone could in my circumstances. I knew I was a child of God, but it was not long until I became fully conscious that there was a deeper work of grace needed within me. My parents both professed entire sanctification at the time of the conversion of the four oldest children, which included myself, but my life was much occupied in securing an education, and having but limited opportunities I was absorbed mostly with my studies, then afterward became engaged in educational work for a number of years. It needed no arguments to prove that my parents possessed a deeper spiritual life than I did, and although the doctrine of sanctification was not so clearly taught and understood then as now, yet I was fully aware this was what I needed. Sometimes I thought I had obtained the experience, but soon it was proved by unmistakable evidence that I was not sanctified. I had not come to the point of a definite and absolute consecration, and really did not understand how to make this consecration. My great ambition in life was to make a mark in the world. This was so deeply implanted within me that I caused every energy to bend in that direction. I dearly loved God and fully realized my utter dependence upon him, but my love was not perfected. Then unfortunately I had a quick temper, which I found justification had not destroyed. It was materially repressed and generally held under control, but it was there and needed only the provocation to assert its presence; and sometimes, I am sorry to say, it brought me under condemnation and I had cause to repent and regain the sweet peace of God.

But the manner of my life, I believe, as a whole, was such that none of my most intimate acquaintances had any reason to question the sincerity of my heart or my profession as a Christian. The one who was most dissatisfied with my inward condition was myself, and for more than eight years I knew that a deeper work must be wrought before I could be satisfied. Oh, how truly I could understand the prayer of David when he so longed for a clean heart; and had I been brought to the knowledge of the complete consecration, I might have been living in this blessed Canaan rest of soul soon after my conversion. But God was good and full of tender mercy. He carried me along and forgave my defeats and so lovingly bore with me, even though my heart was divided between him and some things of this world. I had forsaken all that I had to follow Jesus, but unconsciously these objects would come between Jesus, the object of my love, and myself, and thus hinder the perfect communion of the Holy Spirit. About one year prior to my entering into this perfect rest, the doctrine of sanctification was quite thoroughly agitated. Some advocates of the Zinzendorf doctrine produced some strong efforts to overthrow the doctrine of the second work of grace. I had studied the scriptures carefully and honestly, and while I did not have the experience of the second grace myself, I was certain that the one-work teaching was not correct; for I knew I had received all that my heart could receive in the grace of pardon, and knew also that I soon found that I needed just exactly what the term sanctification implies, and what the dear ones who believed in and were advocating the second work of grace were testifying to by word and deed.

In the winter of 1883-4, while dear companion and myself were engaged with some sanctified ones in a protracted meeting, to rescue the perishing, we were brought as never before face to face with the stern necessity of more spiritual power and life. We were shown by the Holy Spirit that there is but one route to the promised land and that is by crossing the Jordan. Death was inevitable if we would come into this abundant life. We paused and reflected, looked backward and forward, but there was no alternative--death was our doom. One day while I was absent from home, and dear companion was left alone, the Lord spoke to her so plainly that she had one cherished idol that must necessarily be sacrificed. It was a God-given blessing, but must be yielded freely to him. She obeyed and entered into the glory of sanctification. When I returned home I soon found that the work in her was done. Something marvelous had been accomplished. It was wonderful what a change. She told me of the death she had to pass through and I fully realized it. The divine glory which had come into her heart was unspeakable. She tried to show me how to die the same death. I was desirous to yield and cross over with her, but I found a resistance in my will which held me back. I came to my cherished treasures, some of which were God-given blessings, but unquestionably the Holy Spirit said they must be yielded up a burnt offering unto the Lord. My will must become swallowed up into the will of God completely, even to this death. I said, "Yes, Lord, I will"; but the yes found a hesitancy. It did not reach the depths of my heart. I kept saying it over and over--"Yes, Lord"--and tried to get it deeper every time I said it; but the Lord knew it did not reach the inmost depths. That was a wonderful day to me, but it was not the day of my death, as it was of my companion. She told in meeting that evening what the Lord had wrought. I told what I was trying to say to the Lord--"Thy will be done."

Time passed by and I still hesitated. I wanted the Lord's perfect will, but also wanted just a little of my will. I wanted both, but the Lord showed that I could have but one; and I plainly knew which one, if I was ever to obtain the grace of sanctification. The life of my companion was a daily testimony which only added to my trouble. I knew she had what she never had before. Her life before was all that I ever expected to find in a true, devoted, Christian woman, but now in some marvelous manner there was vastly more heaven in her life than before, and the marked absence of everything unlike heaven. I knew she was sanctified, and I knew I was not. She had just what I must have, and what my soul was longing for these years. Oh, why could I not just now say "Yes!" with my whole heart and die the death and gain the abundant life? Sometimes I was under such conviction that I felt miserable. I asked God to forgive me for not yielding up my whole heart as I knew he would have me do.

* * * * *

Weeks and months passed and my attention became absorbed in business and the cares of life, but these months were more unsatisfactory than all my previous Christian life, and some of this time I certainly lived on a very low plane of spirituality, and it is evident that I at last came to the point where my justification would have been forfeited had I not gone over and possessed the land. I struggled and suffered sometimes unutterably. After the struggle was over and I was sanctified I could look back and see where I had come up to a deep chasm so deep and dark that I could not see the bottom. It was too wide for me to step across. On the other side was everything my soul longed for. I could see the beautiful plane and way of sanctification. My loved ones were walking on it and rejoicing in its glory. Above the chasm there seemed suspended a rope securely fastened and strong enough to hold my weight, and it seemed that I could easily take hold of this rope and by a desperate effort swing myself across the chasm. I had taken hold of the rope and was for a long time hesitating about making the leap. The chasm was the depth I must drop into in order to reach sanctification, but it seemed awful--so deep and dark, and no assurance that I would ever see life again. The rope was my will. I had presumed to swing across without going into the death, but God knew that would not be his way, and there I stood, gazing with fear and trembling into the immensity of this dark chasm into which to leap meant certain death. Later I had taken hold of the rope and swung myself away from where I had been standing, with the hope of reaching the other side. I could not reach it and now was worse off than before, for I was now suspended above the chasm and could neither go back nor go forward. There I was hanging and swinging, holding on for life, and yet the Holy Spirit kept saying, "Let go."

My sufferings increased until I began to feel that death would be a relief. At that time God sent a brother to us who preached a sermon from the text, 1 Peter 4:1, 2, with emphasis upon the clause, "For he that hath suffered in the flesh hath ceased from sin." The Holy Spirit applied this to me and revealed to my soul the utter necessity of death to gain sanctification. The end came, I let go my death grip of the rope and said as I never said before, "Yes, Lord, thy will be done!" I knew that it reached the uttermost depth of my soul. God knew it, and I am certain that Satan knew it. At the close of that meeting I said, "I am now offered up." There was no conscious change only I knew my will was yielded, and I am certain that not an atom of earth existed between God and me. We went home late in the evening, and as I was retiring I knelt once more before God and simply told him that now after these months of struggle it was all ended and I was so thankful to him that I could say so sweetly, "Thy will be done." My hold upon the rope had become so weary. How sweet and blessed now to rest so securely in that infinite will. The great chasm was deep and dark, but I was so glad that I had let go and dropped into it; for I was so conscious now that even in the darkness and depths I was in his will. As I dropped, loving arms of Jesus had caught me and I was glad to be in death with him. I felt within me that something wonderful was about to take place. I arose from my knees and scarcely had time to lie down when truly I experienced a taste of death. Wholly unconscious of my earthly surroundings, but knowing I was in the presence of Jesus, I believe a death was wrought within me, after which the baptism of pentecostal fire and the Holy Ghost came upon me. The refining fire went through my very body and the effect seemed terrible. The sublime consciousness of the presence of heaven and the majesty of God was such as mortal tongue can never describe. Then following the distinct baptism of fire the floodgates of heaven's glory were opened upon me, and, oh, the heavenly deluge that followed can be realized only by those who have experienced the same.

More than sixteen years have passed since this wonderful event, and while the emotions of feeling have been varied through the labors and toils of a busy life (both in business life, and twelve years in the gospel ministry), I can testify to the glory of God that the power and victory in this blessed second grace has been all-sufficient. The word of God, now I found, was full of sanctification, and my new experience spoiled me for any arguments against the doctrine as a second work of grace, and in due time I could plainly see that according to the word of God and the plan of redemption it must be an experience subsequent to justification. The conscious presence of the indwelling Holy Spirit and the knowledge of a pure heart in this precious grace is what we need continually in this battle against the powers of the enemy.

Brother and sister, have you had your Pentecost? If not, tarry at Jerusalem. "And the very God of peace sanctify you wholly; and I pray God your whole spirit and soul and body be preserved blameless unto the coming of our Lord Jesus Christ. Faithful is he that calleth you, who also will do it."--1 Thess. 5:23, 24.

* * * * *

Transcriber's Note

Minor punctuation errors have been corrected without notice. A few obvious typographical errors have been corrected and are listed below.

Page 3: "The Holy Spirit of Promise" page number changed from "23" to "25".

Page 8: "It is indispensible" changed to "It is indispensable".

Page 17: "the words "having" signifying" changed to "the word "having" signifying".

Page 36: "than should no place" changed to "then should no place".

Page 45: "so deeply inbedded" changed to "so deeply embedded".

Page 62: "of ecclestiastical bondage" changed to "of ecclesiastical bondage".

Page 62: "will in every individaul" changed to "will in every individual".

Page 63: "throughly furnished unto all" changed to "thoroughly furnished unto all".

Pages 77-78: "made "perfect his death" changed to "made "perfect" by his death".

Page 85: "sanctificed condition" changed to "sanctified condition".

Page 90: "Chapter XIV" changed to "Chapter XIII".

Page 95: "no consicous change only" changed to "no conscious change only".

CPSIA information can be obtained at www.ICGtesting.com
Printed in the USA
LVOW04s2243191015

458874LV00031B/776/P

9 781507 542804